THE TWO-CAREER MARRIAGE

CHRISTIAN CARE BOOKS

Wayne E. Oates, Editor

1 When Your Parents Divorce
  William V. Arnold

2 When the Mental Patient Comes Home
  George Bennett

3 Coping with Physical Disability
  Jan Cox-Gedmark

4 After Suicide
  John H. Hewett

5 The Two-Career Marriage
  G. Wade Rowatt, Jr., and Mary Jo Rowatt

6 Coping with Difficult People
  Paul F. Schmidt

COVERING BOOKS 1–6

Pastor's Handbook, Vol. I
  Wayne E. Oates

THE
TWO–CAREER MARRIAGE

by

G. Wade Rowatt, Jr.

and

Mary Jo Brock Rowatt

THE WESTMINSTER PRESS
Philadelphia

Scripture quotations from the Revised Standard
Version of the Bible are copyrighted 1946, 1952, ©
1971, 1973 by the Division of Christian Education of
the National Council of the Churches of Christ in
the U.S.A., and are used by permission.

BOOK DESIGN BY DOROTHY ALDEN SMITH

First edition

Published by The Westminster Press®
Philadelphia, Pennsylvania

PRINTED IN THE UNITED STATES OF AMERICA
9 8 7 6 5 4 3 2 1

Library of Congress Cataloging in Publication Data

Rowatt, Wade.
  The two-career marriage.

  (Christian care books ; 5)
  Bibliography: p.
  1. Marriage—United States. 2. Married people—
Employment—United States. I. Rowatt, Mary Jo Brock,
1943–   joint author. II. Title. III. Series.
HQ536.R68   306.8   79–28408
ISBN 0–664–24298–7

To John Brock and Wade Clinton

Our source of joy
in the delightful world of parenthood
and dual careers

Contents

Preface   9

1. HELP! WE'RE BOTH EMPLOYED!   11

   Where Does It Hurt? *13*
   Where Have Others Hurt? *19*
   Where Are We Employed? *23*
   Where Do We Go from Here? *24*

2. WHAT'S IN IT FOR US?   26

   Financial Advantages *26*
   Family Assets *28*
   Freedom Advancements *32*
   Growth Options *36*

3. WHOSE CHILDREN ARE THESE?   41

   Children Have a Right to a Mother *43*
   Children Have a Right to a Father *45*
   Pregnancy Can Be a Problem *46*
   Child-Care Alternatives Vary Widely *48*
   Homework and Those First Few Minutes
       After School *51*

Identity Formation of the Child
    Is a Role Issue *53*
Childhood Illness and Developmental
    Stress *55*

4. WHO DOES THE DIRTY WORK?   58

Two Persons Versus Three Jobs *61*
Sort Out the Dirty Work *64*
Spread Out the Dirty Work *66*
Farm Out the Dirty Work *69*

5. WHERE DOES ALL THE TIME GO?   72

Dual-Career Time Demands *74*
Daily Time Demands *78*
The Passing of the Years *83*

6. HOW DO YOU TELL THE MEN
    FROM THE WOMEN?   87

Can a Woman Do a "Man's" Job? *89*
Can a Man Do a "Woman's" Job? *92*
Equal Pay for Equal Work? *95*
Power and Sex Roles *96*
Same-Profession Couples *98*

7. THE CHURCH'S RESPONSE
    TO EMPLOYED COUPLES   102

Focus on Family Life *103*
Examining Our Own House *106*
Church Programs for Employed
    Couples *109*

Bibliography   115

Preface

Employed couples experience unique pressures in contemporary society. Some of these pressures grow out of their decision that both shall enter the labor market and at the same time maintain a relationship as partners. Family stress increases if the dual-career couple also has children. Other pressures come from the social context. Social values both encourage and inhibit dual careers.

We address the special problem areas of spouses who both work outside the home, and we attempt to offer some alternatives for creative growth. This book does not pretend to be *the* model for employed couples but rather suggests guidelines by which each couple can transform their career duels into a mutually constructive pattern for dual careers.

Through the pages of this book a subtle message recurs as a guiding principle for couples who strive for growth. Growth for dual-career dyads comes only when each partner knows her or his own pain and feels something of the hurt of the other, and then *they* seek creative alternatives. In their search for models, dual-career couples must break through narrow patriarchal dominance and hostile, radical feminism to a fuller vision of what it means to be human.

9

We acknowledge and confess our Christian bias in suggesting that a two-way covenant between married partners must be at the heart of dual-career growth. For us, theological models have been powerful symbols in our growth as a working couple. When each person values the other and knows that only in grace can one be acceptable, the career duels can be transformed into growth. We do not suggest a conflict-free model, but we encourage couples to face conflict openly and honestly.

We are especially thankful to Wayne E. Oates, our teacher, friend, colleague, and editor, for his faithful assistance from conception to completion of this volume. He lures us forward by his loving relationship with Pauline as together they have respected each other's right to be individuals.

Our thanks go out to Charlotte Ellen and Howard J. Clinebell, who during a year of study leave have been our teachers by word and deed.

Without the support of a sabbatical leave from the Southern Baptist Theological Seminary for Wade and a special leave of absence from the Greater Clark County Schools for Jodi, this book would never have happened. We thank our employers for their creative support as the kind of administrators that encourage growth beyond the walls of their institutions.

Our hope is that this book will be a growth experience for couples and those who are committed to help them.

G.W.R., Jr.
M.J.B.R.

1. Help!
We're Both Employed!

Visions of a warm summer evening walk by a mountain lake filled our daydreams. Naively, we promised never to let this honeymoon end. We had been married seven days and were ready to live blissfully ever after. As excited newlyweds, we sped across plains and around curves toward our first home. Actually, the campus apartment was tiny and cramped.

Our young-love fantasies collided with the reality of building a nest. As we unloaded our household equipment—mostly still cluttered with gift wrap, wedding rice, and bows—Wade began to theorize. "I promise always to provide for you economically. Don't worry; you will never have to work," he crowed. By "work" he meant, of course, "be gainfully employed outside our home."

This statement being interpreted by Jodi (Mary Jo) meant, He doesn't expect me to work to put him through school—even though I'm willing to do so. A bit surprised, Jodi sighed, "Fine, I'm tired of school and of work." She had worked part time to help put herself through college. Since she had graduated only two weeks earlier, she chirped, "I'll enjoy fixing up our apartment, cooking, cleaning, and just supporting you in your goals."

11

This conversation as interpreted by Wade meant, Oh boy! I have a girl just like the girl who married dear old Dad. Wade envisioned a traditional marriage and Jodi agreed.

The myth lasted one week. Jodi announced, "I've arranged and rearranged the kitchen and all our furniture. I'm bored. I want to take an evening-school class."

Wade was shocked. Thoughts flashed rapidly across his mind's screen. What's wrong? Where have I failed? My mother never had to take an evening class because she was bored.

Before he could protest, Jodi continued to bubble: "There is a class on the 'Role of the Minister's Wife' that really sounds interesting."

Wade was relieved and thought, Oh how nice, she wants to learn more about helping me be a success. He eagerly replied, "Why not? That sounds like a great idea."

Jodi later uncovered her young husband's bias. Wade did not want her ever to be employed outside their home. She enrolled as a full-time student six months into their union. Just prior to their third anniversary both spouses graduated with their master's degrees—ready for the job market. By choice Jodi has worked mostly part time for the ten years since then. Wade has worked mostly full time ever since.

We alternatively have cried out, "Help! We're both employed! What can we do about this stress? How can we relieve the pressure?" Still, the strain has seemed a better alternative than either of us giving up our self-expression and ministry through work. Jodi has worked as a music therapist, church organist, and teacher. Wade has been an assistant pastor, pastor, hospital chaplain, pastoral counselor, and seminary professor. Each of these positions has been balanced, at times juggled, with duties as husband and wife, father and mother.

As we look around we notice numerous other couples suffering the stress and reaping the rewards of dual-career marriages. In blending the gains from our pilgrimage with current research, we intend that your hurt might be eased and your gains multiplied. In Chapter 2 we'll discuss more of the rewards of a dual-career marriage, but often the rewards come after some pain.

Where Does It Hurt?

The sources of stress vary when a husband and wife are both gainfully employed. The sources multiply when children are present. At times the marriage "hurts all over." An overview of the hurting areas can bring order from the chaos. Major tension areas for us have included an array of problems.

First there was the question, Whose job has priority? Since we had both graduated in May, we were ready to work at the same time. Jodi was offered a full-time position as a music therapist in a psychiatric institution where she had trained during her last semester. Wade was called to a church over a thousand miles away. With only a bit of discussion about the benefits of music therapy, Jodi obediently resigned and we moved. When we married, Jodi had expected that she would follow wherever Wade's work led.

However, the matter did not end there. Once again feeling bored and confined in the house within a couple of months, Jodi had difficulty finding a suitable position. She applied to do substitute teaching and ran from school to school for half a year. She finally finished the semester teaching in an area outside either her major or minor areas; a teacher was ill and could not finish the year. Jodi was unfulfilled, frustrated, and disappointed. Wade felt angry, aggravated, and grieved that she "could not find her place and settle down." He even felt a bit of guilt that she had been forced to leave a satisfying position. The first year neither partner won, and the marriage did not win in the move because of the stress between our two career needs. A year later, when Jodi found meaningful employment, the stress abated considerably.

We would perhaps move again if faced with a similar situation, but not as casually. Certainly we would discuss more fully our feelings, hopes, and personal goals. Neither of us would demand that the other move for a new position or stay because of our present job. Our dual-career marriage for a time had become a career duel!

As long as we squirmed and strove over whose job came first, our marriage suffered. The stress grew from our having a parent-to-child relationship between us as husband and wife. We both felt much better about treating each other, and being treated, as adults.

A *second* area of hurt focused around Wade's daily question, "Why isn't dinner ready?" This question centered around role expectations. When Jodi returned from class or work only minutes before Wade, time wasn't sufficient to prepare a meal. Eventually, Jodi discovered several prepared-ahead menus, but as this issue grew, old basic assumptions conflicted. Wade had relented on the issue of Jodi being employed for personal fulfillment on one unspoken assumption. Of course, she would still do *all* of the cooking, cleaning, shopping, mending, and washing!

Jodi, on the other hand, contended that if she helped "bring home the bacon," then Wade could help cook it and even help clean up afterward. The results have been an inconsistent reshuffling of domestic duties. At times we have shared, almost equally, total household responsibilities. At other times when Wade worked sixty hours a week, Jodi continued to carry major responsibility for engineering the house. Wade has found certain tasks rewarding. Since his family operated a laundromat as he grew up, he thinks he is a whiz at washing clothes. The food isn't half bad when he sticks to his limited menus. Still, he isn't compulsive enough to pass inspection as a house cleaner. Neither of us delights in certain jobs, but we force ourselves to the task at hand.

The stress of reshuffling chores far exceeded the stress of maintaining our new routines. Sharing domestic tasks wasn't as bad as getting used to the idea. The idea of shared home care violated ideals deeply ingrained by traditional culture. With the passing of time this stress also diminished.

A *third* area of frustration voiced itself in the cry, "We just can't get it all done tonight!" Time was a factor. Each evening was packed with chores from a long and expanding list of "things to do today." An increasing number of normal housekeeping jobs were left undone. Trying to balance three full-time occupations, one being housekeeping, between two persons meant leaving something up in the air. The sheer volume of work to be done exceeded the time and energy of two human beings. We felt like two clowns trying to perform simultaneously in three circus rings. We were tired, fatigued, and drained. The rat races at our places of employment were exhausting by themselves. Adding daily home routines was just too much.

We modified our habits and routines somewhat. Furthermore, we lowered our expectations. The house, lawn, and car are not absolutely perfect most of the time. After years of practice, balancing three roles can still be tricky.

We were both shocked recently when one of our offspring asked compassionately: "Daddy, what day is the work you are doing?" Quite puzzled, Wade replied, "This is today and I'm doing my work today. What do you mean?"

"I mean what day's work is this? Mommy has been doing *yesterday's* work all day!" he sympathetically reported!

Perhaps you find yourself behind in the day's work well into each night. Adjusting to a new division of labor and modifying routines can help reduce the long-range stress. After an intensive study of 560 households, one sociologist concluded that only minor differences exist in the stress levels of wives who had been working full time for more than one year and in wives who had never been employed outside their homes. More surprisingly, he discovered a slight tendency for husbands of dual-career couples to be happier and under less stress than men who were married to full-time housewives (Booth, p. 649). This study does indicate that some rewards exist if a wife starts to work.

Fourth, stress came from feeling that we were in a rut. "Can we take a vacation next year?" became an annual question for several consecutive years. We were too busy to stop to play. Rest, relaxation, replenishment, and recreation were squeezed from our lives by the choking hand of hard work. We had become hooked on labor. Wayne Oates's apt term applied to us: we were "workaholics," persons addicted to work (Oates, *Confessions of a Workaholic,* p. 4). We had a tent but camped only once or twice a year. We had rusty fishing equipment, unmarred tennis rackets, and sparkling golf balls. Our little boat spent so much time in the garage we marveled that it remembered how to "swim" on its once- or twice-yearly trip to the lake.

Of course, we suffered as persons. "All work and no play . . ." You probably know all too well how that goes. A lack of relaxation strains the human system. The sabbath principle of a work-rest cycle cannot be violated without grave consequences.

Correspondingly, little time was found or made for spiritual replenishment. Oh, we hurriedly made it to church at least once a week, but that hardly sufficed. Time for personal reflection, daily meditation, and family worship was nearly nonexistent. We lived off the reserves from our heritage as religious beings. Losing the vital resource of worshipful living added to the pressure we experienced as a dual-career couple.

Fifth, stress came from being isolated from peers. "Guess who's coming to dinner" held no meaning for us. We could not get off the treadmill long enough for guests. Meals were fitted into the packed schedule wherever a few minutes could be found. Visitors were a rarity. Except for one or two couples—with whom we *worked,* of course—we were alone in our rapid rush for self-expression.

Wade *expected* Jodi to invite his friends and their wives, plan a multi-course meal, and arrange for an enjoyable evening at least every other week. Naturally, Wade was too busy to help much. In fact, things got so hectic at one point that Wade called from an airport five hundred miles up the flight path to report a delay. The former boss and his wife had already arrived! Dinner was only three hours late and these friends understood everything. The man willingly accepted our embarrassed apology and added, "I know how those things happen." Then we realized that he really did understand. He and his wife are both involved in full-time remunerative work!

Sixth, and perhaps most importantly, stress comes from questions of child care and family demands. "Whose children are these?" asked Jodi.

"Why, of course, they are *ours,* but you take care of them most of the time," Wade responded.

"Why do I always have to find a sitter when we decide at the last minute to take time for a night out together?" Jodi continued. Well, from then on, even securing a sitter has been a dual task.

However, for us child care was not a dueling affair. Partly from early expectations and partly by necessity Wade eagerly enlisted for child-care duty. Wade's father had spent a lot of time with his sons. He would be the only father playing ball in a backyard filled with children. Naturally, Wade expected to play with and enjoy the children.

Unexpectedly, our first child was followed by a second little blessing. The twins, then, needed twice as much attention as one child would. We were miles from relatives, so we both "mothered" them. We sat up nights, each feeding a baby, or arose early to make enough formula for the next twenty-four hours. Both babies even seemed to need a clean diaper at the same time, so we each did our part. Out of the stress came a blessing; Wade learned the joy of a close relationship to children *before* they were big enough to toss a football. A stronger father-child bond can be a positive spin-off for employed parents.

Nevertheless, child-related stress did abound even after we moved. Who would care for them while Jodi worked even a few hours a week? What could we do when one contracted chicken pox and could not go to the child-care center? We were ready with a helpful aunt when the other one came down sick three days after the first recovered. Nevertheless, what if your mother cannot come? What did we do when we both had evening extras for the job tomorrow? Who bathed the children and tucked them into bed?

As you can see, we are not writing this book as an academic exercise. We are not standing above the press box to call out plays for an end run around the stress of working couples. We plan to intertwine our experiences with recent research and current situations of other couples we have interviewed. Stress in the lives of other employed spouses stretches the areas of pain even further.

Where Have Others Hurt?

The literature and our conversations have pointed out at least four other areas of pain for two-career couples. The husband and wife often feel the stress of wives being in the jungle of business pressure. Delinquency has, at times, been blamed on "working mothers." Divorce is rising and dual-career couples' duels receive much of the blame. Finally, when both spouses work, how the money is spent can be a problem. Married women feel the pressure for exceedingly superior performance on their jobs. Otherwise, they are passed over for promotions. When a married male was promoted over an equally qualified female, the excuse given was poor. Ignoring the fact that the male was a husband and a father, the boss said, "She has her first commitment to her family, and he can be free to give more outside time to the company." Husbands of working women frequently feel furious when their wives are treated unjustly.

One study has indicated that managerial attitudes are even less positive toward husbands whose wives work than toward employees whose spouses do not work outside the home (Rosen, Jerdee, and Prestwich, p. 565).

Opponents of working mothers sometimes blame juvenile delinquency totally on employed wives. Millie began to work when her husband became seriously ill. At first the family rallied around to aid with work at home and to ease her heavy load. When it became evident that Fred might be permanently disabled, the family lost much of its hope. For a few years Fred and Millie were employed, but he worked less and less. Their thirteen-year-old son turned to street activities, staying out later and later. The son was involved in minor difficulty before the parents realized what was happening. Later Millie blamed herself for their son's misfortunes.

Although delinquency among youth tends to be blamed on working parents, this cause has not been validated by the research. "Most studies find no significant differences in the emotional adjustment of the children of employed mothers, either when the children are young . . . or during adolescence" (Udry, p. 307). However, new evidence points to a belief that the effect of a mother working may have positive effects for girls and negative effects for boys. Another study found that the sons have adjustment difficulty only whenever the mother's employment indicates something about a failure of the father (Udry, p. 307). On the other hand, daughters of working mothers are found to admire their mothers more than daughters of nonworking mothers. The daughters of working mothers have a more clearly formed self-concept than female offspring whose mothers are not remuneratively employed (Udry, p. 307). Children do feel the stress when both parents work; the total effects are not clear.

Sometimes divorce is related to working women. Al, a rather quiet Sunday school teacher, silently lingered on the edge of our conversation group. When the others had left, Al began to speak before he even introduced himself. He indicated that he wanted to talk about a "personal matter." We found a quiet room and he spilled out his hurt, frustration, and confusion. After twenty-two years of marriage, Joyce had returned to school. She now had her first job as a nurse at the local hospital.

Al had disapproved from the beginning, but she protested that life was meaningless since their two children had left the nest. Last week Al reached his limit and *demanded* that Joyce quit work. She said if she had to leave him to continue her work, then she would leave. Now Al was confused. Should he stand up to her or give in on this critical issue? Al was hurt. How could she be so alone since the children had left? Al reminded her that they still had each other. Was he not enough to keep her happy? Al was frustrated. Conflict, upheaval, and disturbances of this nature ran against his grain as a person. Yet he could not ignore this issue. Many times before he dropped the subject when he and Joyce disagreed. In desperation Al voiced the fear of many insecure males. "Working women cause marriages to fail. That's why the divorce rate is so high," Al exclaimed!

Al's oversimplification contains some truth, but the issues extend beyond just work. Listen to the unfolding agony from a woman's side.

"I agree with all this (liberation talk), but it's scary! What do you do when you realize after ten years of marriage and two kids that either you have to leave or you die inside? I kept hoping that my husband would see the reasonableness of my wanting things different. He didn't. He wanted the woman he married—the straight housewife-mother—so now I'm a divorcée. In spite of that *awful* word, I'm a lot freer and happier person. But I'd like to know if it's possible to make it with a man and remain a human being" (Charlotte H. Clinebell, *Counseling for Liberation*, p. 7).

One real dimension of working couples focuses on the potential for divorce during the painful adjustments. A simple cause-effect relationship has not been established, but marital breakup haunts many dual-career spouses.

Money becomes the focus for some couples. The two-paycheck couple that focuses only on the economic side of their joint venture soon resembles a corporation with only two board members. Feminist Caroline Bird has discussed the dual-career couple from the economic perspective in her new paperback *The Two-Paycheck Marriage*. Placing the emphasis on the economic side of marriage does create many problems that lead some to conclude that the future of the "husband, wife, and children" model for the family is questionable. We disagree with this position and suggest that the problem is as much with the focus on economics of the two-career family as with the family as an institution.

We will propose throughout this volume that a few key issues, not economic in nature, are the keys to understanding dual-career families. *Commitment* is the major factor for dual-career couples facing career duels. The couple's commitment to each other strengthens the relationship. The parents' commitment to any children they bring into the world undergirds their struggles to solve child-care problems. The family's commitment to society at large provides a sense of direction and values. *Freedom* is a related factor for dual-career homes. Wives need the freedom to choose to be solely homemakers, to combine this role with volunteer activities, or to work for pay. Husbands need the freedom to be family members emotionally and not just economically. Children need the freedom to become persons and to have parents dedicated to that task.

Where Are We Employed?

Yes, the one who works for pay is employed, whether in an office at home or somewhere outside the home. In a different sense of the word the homemaker is employed; that is, the housewife, homemaker, or "domestic engineer" is used or advantageously occupied in work. In still another sense of the word a volunteer worker is employed by devoting or directing attention to a particular activity, a person, or persons.

We want to avoid assigning relative values to the decisions of a person to be a homemaker, an "employee," or a volunteer, or some combination of these possibilities. Each choice has worth and is to be valued. Surely, the worth of homemaking and of parenting, which is so often assumed to be an integral part of homemaking, is rightly esteemed.

A person who works, though without pay, by volunteering and giving oneself can do and donate so much as to be considered a full-time volunteer. Many people and organizations benefit from volunteers' generosity. The total hours of volunteered time given to individuals and groups of people in homes, churches, schools, hospitals, service clubs, and political and civic organizations must be enormous. A "career volunteer" could well feel the pressures of household maintenance as much as a person who works for pay. A person who is gainfully employed half time and also a volunteer half time could also feel these pressures. Unpaid work outside the home does deserve affirmation.

Our point is not to assign values to homemaking, volunteering, or working for pay. Rather, we seek to address the problems and possibilities that could be encountered by career volunteers as well as paycheck persons. Since more hours of out-of-the-home work are paid than volunteered, the discussion will most often be slanted toward those working for pay.

Where Do We Go from Here?

The preceding pages have painted an awesome picture of the stress on working couples. Why do a man and a woman both work? They find many rewards with the frustrations. In fact, for centuries neither husbands nor wives worked outside the home. The home was a cave, a tent, a farm, or a shop where work was concentrated. For a clear image of woman's equality as a person even in the time of Jesus, see

Evelyn and Frank Stagg's detailed study *Woman in the World of Jesus.*

Chapter 2 focuses on the positive side of dual-career marriages. If this stress is so great, some rewards must be present. Indeed, advantages do exist for working wives, their husbands, and their marriages.

Can children survive relatively unharmed when their parents work? Will these children create a fresh new society with revitalized churches? Do the female offspring of laboring parents have a lasting advantage? These and other child-related issues will be explored in Chapter 3.

Who does the jobs nobody else wants to do? How do the routine, dull, grinding tasks get divided? Who does the dirty work? Chapter 4 sorts through a multitude of questions related to the total division of labor.

How do working couples find time to live a normal life? What if they work different hours or separate shifts? The family needs time, but where do they locate even one spare hour? Time management disputes spring up in Chapter 5.

With women taking over more jobs, what is left as a man's work? Can a *lady* be a truck driver? Do real men do the wash and feed the baby? The question of role reversal and sex-role-related events engage the reader in Chapter 6.

Do Christians get involved in the dynamics of these problems? Can the church help the multitude of suffering, working couples? What can one church do for its community? What can dual-career couples do to help their churches be more effective? The concluding chapter zeroes in on these queries and offers hope for the despairing, joy for the depressed, faith for the disbelieving, and love for the disturbed spouses.

2. What's in It for Us?

You might be wondering why in over 50 percent of American marriages both spouses are employed. Perhaps you have even asked, "Why are we both working? Why do we keep this up?" With all of the stresses mentioned in the first chapter, dual careers might seem not possible, practical, or palatable, and certainly not pleasant. Dual careers do not have to result in career duels. Couples who learn to call off the dueling can find dual careers an attractive alternative. In exploring "What's in it for us," couples have discovered a vast, rich, green oasis of rewards, benefits, and bonuses. In fact, we have uncovered quite a list of rewards for couples who work outside of their home.

FINANCIAL ADVANTAGES

The advantages of two incomes for personal and family support has launched many wives into the orbit of the employment sphere. Relief from mounting monthly payments, double-digit annual inflation, and the media's advertising pressure lures couples of *all ages* into dual careers. For some, having two incomes seems to be the only option. Most couples slide into the both-working category for economic relief, but remain for a multitude of reasons.

Financial gains can provide the husband an opportunity for further education. More than a few wives work to put "hubby" through school. His education is supposed to prepare him for a better-paying job, but she frequently continues to work long after the celebrated graduation date. Even if they move, both tend to seek employment.

The newly marrieds work so they can buy homemaking necessities, purchase a house, or afford special recreational equipment. Couples are more on their own now than in previous generations because of family mobility and declining extended-family networks. This fact, linked with the skyrocketing cost of housing, paints a brighter picture for maintaining dual careers. Many couples seem to expect to begin their marriage at or above the standard set by their parents after years of acquiring. Two paychecks make this possible in many instances.

By the time a couple has reached the middle years, the economic benefits of joint employment meet different needs but are still welcomed. Median adults desire extra income for more sophisticated, expensive, recreational appetites. Skis, tennis racquets, golf clubs, and bicycles are dropped from their want lists in favor of items like summer cottages, recreational vehicles, Holy Land tours, exotic vacations, children's college expenses, and original art works.

The desire for more prestigious living usually leads to investing extra dollars in a larger dwelling, fine furniture, designer clothing, and at least one extra automobile. The couple's tastes have changed since they first established housekeeping.

Furthermore, the financial benefits enable a couple to save for their own retirement, help with their youth's educational expenses, and perhaps assist aging parents who live on a fixed income. In general, economic advantages emancipate a couple for a more giving life-style.

However, we must enter a word of caution at this point. Not all of a second income is strictly extra. Additional expenses accompany that second income. Perhaps higher-bracket taxes will gobble up a disproportionate amount. Child care for young children could consume a large portion. Transportation can take a big bite. Household help, convenience foods, restaurant eating, additional clothing, and indiscriminate shopping all eat into the extra income. In spite of these limitations on a second salary, the monetary gains are worth it for most working couples. An array of other good reasons for maintaining two careers can be given.

FAMILY ASSETS

In addition to the economic advantages already discussed, the family grows emotionally when both parents work. Although stress increases, the stress need not be destructive. Like heat in a car engine or a kitchen oven, the right amount of stress can be productive. Some of the family assets accumulated from the stress of dual employment help the children while others aid the parents, but generally the entire family grows.

The assets on the children's side of the ledger center around developmental advantages. Although infants need close attachment and long periods with their mothers and/ or fathers, preschool and elementary school children of working parents grow emotionally from socialization opportunities at child-care centers. This broadening experience seems much better than being alone with a frustrated, preoccupied parent who lives for the day he or she can return to the employment scene.

Much has been said about the role of fathers in determining the positive self-image of sons. However, as mothers develop their careers, daughters gain in their self-image also. Girls of working mothers admire their mothers more, have a more flexible projected role for themselves, and generally have a less passive and self-degrading concept of themselves. Jodi respects the model her father and mother set as they loved and cared for each family member while engaging in dual careers. Moreover, it appears that boys do not suffer from their mother's employment unless it is accompanied by a father's failure as a family leader (Udry, p. 307).

Children are more likely to join in routine chores around the home if both parents are working outside the home. Not only do they develop a wholesome attitude about labor but they learn valuable skills for later living. Boys and girls learn more about home, lawn, and car care when they join in the family's work routines.

The assets on the parents' side of this family ledger are couple-centered. If both parents work, they are better prepared to face the empty nest when children no longer live at home. Mothers especially become so involved in the lives and activities of their offspring that life seems meaningless after the fledglings "fly off" on their own. The average couple has about half their married life together in the years after the last child has left home. Couples are better prepared for the richness of this period if they have not focused entirely on their children. Howard J. Clinebell suggests that homemakers may turn to outside employment after the children are gone (Howard J. Clinebell, *Growth Counseling for Mid-Years Couples,* p. 67); however, having an existing career, full or part time, eases the entire transition.

A recent cartoon is all too true for some mothers who wait to break into the job market. An interviewer replied to a middle-aged applicant: "So you have kept house for twenty-six years and raised four children. When was the last time you really worked?"

Generally speaking, marital satisfaction is higher for dual-career couples. They experience less marriage stress and discord. Although a husband and a wife go through a brief period of adjustment when they first enter the dual-career category, research suggests that ultimately the wife's employment has beneficial effects on the husband and, therefore, on the marriage.

Further, when both spouses are gainfully employed, one is less likely to become overly dependent on the children. Typically, a mother who spends all her time at home becomes emotionally dependent on her children. Her husband may begin to feel like an outsider in the family system. When both parents work, both may become equally involved with the children and are free for mutual need satisfaction with each other. When careers are dual, then parenting and coupling are more likely to be dual endeavors as well. It seems to us that working parents share more quality time as a pair than do couples with one partner primarily attached to the children. Of course, the children cannot be neglected by working parents without serious consequences. The key is for dual-career couples to balance time together and time with the children. If only the father works away from the home and the mother has the major parenting load dumped on her, then the couple's relationship likely suffers. An additional overdependency of the mother on the children is more likely avoided when both parents are employed.

Consider the negative example of a young couple who came for counseling recently. Flo is thirty-one, a high school graduate, and the mother of three active children (a son, age eleven, and two daughters, ages eight and six). She has never been gainfully employed. Her husband, Henry, age thirty-three, manages a large department store, works long hours six days a week, but provides well for his family. Henry reads the paper on Sunday morning while the family goes to church, and watches television Sunday afternoon and all evenings that he is not working. He reserves one night each month to take "Flo and the kids" to a movie. On Saturday she drives him to work so she and the kids can have the car for grocery shopping and running errands.

Henry was shocked when Flo announced that she wanted a divorce. "What else could you expect?" he retorted. "You have a fine house, three beautiful children, and enough money to pay the bills," he barked proudly.

"Right," she whipped back, "and I can have all those things after we divorce. What else do I want?" she echoed. "I'll tell you!" she almost shouted. "I want a husband! Beautiful children aren't the same as having a marriage partner."

After a period of months during which the couple made an agonizing reevaluation of priorities and a recommitment to each other, Flo added income with a part-time job five mornings a week while the children were in school. Henry hired an assistant manager to relieve the job pressure and cut back his hours. Not all couples resolve such differences even with counseling, but this couple found time together.

FREEDOM ADVANCEMENTS

Freedom, the battle cry of rioting demonstrators of the '60s, has become the personal right of individuals in the '70s. The '80s perhaps will demonstrate how personal freedom is balanced with commitment to family, church, or social group. We feel that each partner must feel personal freedom before being able to fully commit himself or herself to the family. The freedom for self-expression in a vocation liberates a total woman to give more of herself in family interaction. If on the contrary she is enslaved in the home, she cannot feel free to give to her home. Of course, not all homemakers are enslaved, but some who want to work outside the home are opposed by their husbands.

A *sense of personal freedom* gained from dual careers is one major freedom advancement. The wife and the husband both benefit from this gain. Early researchers discovered that the wife's right to choose to work outside and her right to elect to stay at home were equally positive factors in marital happiness. Furthermore, if the husband disapproves of his wife's decision, whether it is to seek employment or to remain primarily a housewife, then the marital adjustment is likely to be lower (Hicks and Platt, pp. 558–559). Although the right to seek outside employment is primarily an advancement in personal freedom for wives, in the last analysis husbands and children gain also. Some couples use the wife's employment as an opportunity for the husband to be primarily a father and homemaker. This situation may be temporary while he returns to school and/or develops skills for a new job or vocation. The option to express oneself in meaningful work grows for both mates. A wife whose husband works can be freer to find self-expressive work than a single woman forced into the job market. In a few cases, working wives have convinced their husbands to become full-time homemakers and they become role-reversed, not dual-career, couples. Sometimes they decide together.

Our interviews did not support the popular opinion that dual-career couples were comprised of a disruptive, hostile woman and a fearful, insecure male. Nevertheless, we did find that domineering, authoritarian husbands contribute to marital unhappiness. Working women sometime seek jobs to escape the control of such a husband.

Perhaps the cartoon circulated in a church-related women's seminar best captured this theme of freedom. A confident, well-groomed, female corporate general manager is flanked by a television interviewing crew. The successful lady executive declares to viewers, "I owe my career to my husband, who inspired me with these words: 'As long as I pay the bills around here, you will do what I say.'"

Adult social interaction while at work is a second major freedom advancement. More than a few housewives and mothers are bored to tears by the lack of adult conversation, interaction, and fellowship. For many hours each day they are isolated in their dwellings with only routine, repetitive, regular, and sometimes revolting chores. Depression, boredom, and even alcoholism attack these imprisoned, segregated, separated human beings. Work outside the home is a social event for them.

A man may take this freedom for granted and may misunderstand his wife's need for adult conversation. However, when threatened with the loss of lunch-hour conversations, coffee-break chats, after-work confabs, and "high level" conferences, men vigorously defend their freedom. They seem to appreciate the presence of women at work but overlook their wives' need for social interaction with their own or the opposite sex.

We are aware that this freedom can be abused with office affairs, on-the-job antics, and "overtime activities." However, this misuse of freedom appears to be no greater for married women than for married men. Single women have long been a part of the employment scene. Unless jobs are sexually segregated, this freedom will continue to be misused by some. That possibility is no reason to keep all wives isolated at home.

A few husbands of employed women were honest enough to admit to us that their main opposition to her starting a job was based on their own insecurity. One minister said bluntly: "I was afraid that she would go to work in the secular community and get interested in another man. Now that I look back I can see how wrong I was, but that is how I felt five years ago."

Freedom from role limitations can be another advancement for both husbands and wives. Role expectations define what is proper and acceptable for a man to do or for a woman to do. Such expectations tend to limit people to performance in specified spheres, allowing them practice and growth only in those spheres, and excluding them from experiences in other areas.

For example, if a husband is expected to be employed forty to sixty or more hours per week, he may become more able and proficient at his work, but he may be excluded or may exclude himself from knowing how to care for the emotional and developmental needs of his children or from performing daily maintenance on his dwelling. On the other hand, a wife and/or mother who only performs at home by cleaning, cooking, mending, etc., may fail to acquire or develop any skills in money management or automobile maintenance; she may even decline in her ability to think and verbalize on the adult level as a result of spending a high percentage of her time in contact only with very young children.

Freedom from role limitations then allows for much more broadening experiences for both males and females. Such liberty allows freedom for crisis adaptability. For example, the husband who has not been isolated from his children but shares deeply in their lives will be better prepared to raise them in the sad event of the loss of their mother. On a shorter-term basis, he would be able to prepare meals, care for clothing, and keep the house from total devastation in the event of the wife's hospitalization or extended illness.

The wife who assumes formerly male roles will likewise be more adaptable in a crisis that incapacitates her husband. In the event of his untimely death she would already have adjusted to the employment scene. Furthermore, her independence in traditionally male areas, such as household repairs and perhaps financial matters, would provide for easier adjustment. In dual careers, couples broaden many areas of personal experience by learning new skills and often by trading off traditional responsibilities. Our point is that such broadening experiences facilitate adjustments in unexpected tragedies. Generally speaking, dual careers offer a couple the freedom to develop a fair division of both opportunities and obligations. While the employment of both spouses does not ensure equity (Rapoport and Rapoport, "Men, Women, and Equity," p. 421) in their relationship and responsibilities, it does generate conditions for liberty to select a fair distribution of responsibilities and to make an optimum allocation of options. Actually, this freedom leads to a fourth area of benefits for dual-career couples—growth.

GROWTH OPTIONS

The women's movement, which has long pressed for options for wives to grow, has generally not emphasized that husbands and marriages can flourish when both spouses are gainfully employed. Research in the early 1960's indicated some adverse effects when married women work. Husbands of working wives told of *significantly* increased marital conflict and reportedly believed that the children would suffer greatly from their mother's absence (Hicks and Platt, p. 558). However, more recent studies have indicated very little difference in the stress level between wives who had worked full time for more than one year and housewives who had never been employed. Furthermore, the wife's outside employment had no significant effect on conjugal bliss or discord. Actually, husbands from dual-career couples enjoyed a happier marriage and were under less stress than men united with housewives (Booth, p. 645). Dual careers not only bring growth for the partners as people and as workers but, when faithfully managed, can generate marital growth. As we discussed earlier, the children can also profit.

Each partner is free to grow as a person when both work,

but employment is obviously not the only factor in personal growth. The case is clear for the wives. Employment is a source of personal growth and satisfaction. Mothers who work full time are more personally satisfied with their work than are full-time housewives. In general, the employed women found life more gratifying than those who remained at home full time (Udry, p. 308).

Personal fulfillment for the working wife may stem from an expanded sense of contribution gained from her job. For centuries, when the home was also an economic center for the family's production, the contributions of a homemaker were more self-evident. However, with the Industrial Revolution and production of goods outside of homes came a certain depreciation of the wife's housekeeping role. Participating in the work force adds economic and creative value to her homemaker image.

These employment benefits have long been taken for granted by men, but some men are discovering additional personal growth when their wives work outside the home. For example, a husband whose wife is gainfully employed is likely to spend more time and energy with the children and less time on any moonlighting jobs. His increased parenting activities create deeper bonds with his own children. Not only does he experience more of their lives, but this contact usually broadens his emotional range. He becomes a more caring, sensitive, emotionally available person. Furthermore, with the discarding of extra part-time work comes more personal time for the couple, which is especially true when both partners work the same hours and are off together. Chapter 5 will develop themes around the time pressures resulting if they report for work on different shifts.

However, when both have jobs outside the home, they are likely to share at least part of the home care. A husband who helps does grow, sometimes painfully, from learning and carrying out household chores. He develops new skills—such as cooking, shopping, and cleaning—and modifies them from his business and work experience.

Each partner can also grow as a capable worker when both have occupations. Since the woman was traditionally barred from the job scene, she grows more from freedom to develop a vocation. A woman who acquires the education, training, and skill for a responsible position but marries and remains at home sees her preparation wasted and watches her abilities slowly fade. On the other hand, one who secures employment develops, refines, and solidifies her skills. She grows as a creator of goods and/or services. Consequently, her creative values expand and reinforce her meaning system. Viktor Frankl, the eminent Viennese psychiatrist, points to creative values as a core reason for finding purposeful living. Having a job gives an added dimension to a woman's self-image. Her self-image is already enhanced by her role as wife, and perhaps mother, but now she is also nurse, secretary, teacher, doctor, truck driver, or executive.

Just as men have long experienced the opportunity for growth as persons on the job, they have for generations had the opportunity for growth as able workers. This growth continues for men whose wives work, but in some cases it is even stronger. When a husband and wife are employed in the same or similar professions, their mutual support seems to push each into a higher level of achievement. One researcher who studied couples employed in the field of psychology concluded that "the husband in professional pairs tends to be extremely productive and perceive decided advantages in his marital situation. . . . Wives in a professional pair tend to be more productive than other females" (Bryson, Bryson, Licht, and Licht, p. 16).

Marital satisfaction can grow when both partners work outside their home. Contrary to popular myth, working wives do not create marital tension, except in the first few months of adjusting to the change. Conflict is a normal by-product of any major change for a couple until the adjustment period (six months or so) is over. Even getting married generates adjustment conflicts at first. One certainly would not lobby against marriage because of adjustment conflict, and we feel the same is true for adjustments to married female employment.

According to recent data, husbands whose wives are employed report more often than husbands of housewives that their mate is just as loving, not more critical, feels better, and has less emotional impairment. A liberal interpretation of this data could conclude that the wife's employment has beneficial effects on the husband and thus on the marriage. If she feels more like a total person, the marriage will grow. A conservative view could at least conclude that a working wife does not harm her marriage (Booth, p. 649).

An earlier study found that from the view of working wives marital satisfaction is higher. Employed married women reported more marital satisfaction than did comparable nonemployed housewives (Safilios-Rothschild, p. 690). This satisfaction was even higher for women with strong commitments to their vocation, according to the same study.

In summary, we have pointed out some of the profound

advantages, assets, growth factors, and options for dual-career couples. When both parents work, the stress, as explained in Chapter 1, is higher but can generate definite benefits for all concerned. We shall now turn our attention specifically to characteristic issues and answers for working couples. The next chapter zeroes in on problems and possibilities of the parents' task when both parents work.

3. Whose Children Are These?

"If you come out of a traditional situation of wife and mother into this," reported a working mother, "there are bound to be times when you feel guilty and there are always people around who will feed that guilt. They say things like 'Who's around to supervise your children after school?' It's their tone of voice, and you know they think you are the worst mother on earth." This sincere mother and wife felt that wondering if she were shortchanging her family was more difficult than the schooling required for her new position (Loper, p. 2).

Another working mother agonized: "Sometimes I've asked myself, 'Is it worth it?' Our children have a lot more chores than other children, and they'll say, 'Well, so-and-so's mother does this and that,' and then I have that—not guilt, but almost sorrow. Am I giving enough to the kids? Every once in a while, I get a chill. Am I going to end up with screwed-up kids?" (Loper, p. 1).

Then there was the incident with a father who dragged his reluctant thirteen-year-old son into Wade's counseling office in Louisville, Kentucky. The father rattled off a long list of symptoms to prove that his son was a real problem for

41

the family. "This boy was an honor student last year but has been cutting classes, smoking on the school campus, tormenting his ten-year-old sister, and even talking back to his mother," complained the father. When Wade asked what the father had tried to do about this situation, he looked surprised and replied, "Well, I brought him to you—I don't have time to mess with him. I work in New England five days a week and am only at home from Saturday morning until Sunday evening. My wife teaches school and is at home by the time they are. Surely you don't think I should be there also!"

The fierce anger of a college freshman still haunts us as we talk with pastors and their spouses. Sherri threw dishes and literally wrecked her apartment at school after she hung up the phone from her father's call. He had explained that due to pressing issues at the church, the family would not be able to come for her first recital as promised. Later in a counseling session, she complained, "My parents were always so wrapped up in helping other people that they forgot about me! Churches should dismiss pastors like my father who neglect their own children!" she bitterly exclaimed.

Jodi, captured by the haunting stare of a frightened eight-year-old neighborhood girl, listened as the little child cautiously asked, "Are you supposed to watch me today?" The child had already checked at the house of another neighbor where she had been instructed by her mother to go after school. "No one was at home over there," she anxiously reported. She had knocked at several houses and could not find an adult who was responsible for her care. Jodi attended to her needs until her mother returned home about an hour later. A confusion in communication had foiled after-school care plans, but all the small girl knew was that she was alone. Although the mothers involved were not employed, they made plans for time away from home similar to arrangements that employed parents must make. Like some children of working couples, the small child was frustrated, afraid, and lonely when she returned from school to an empty house. Children and child care are a major area of adjustment for dual-career parents.

CHILDREN HAVE A RIGHT TO A MOTHER

The understanding love of a mother is an inalienable right of a child (Oates, *On Becoming Children of God,* p. 29). Each infant, born into a mother's waiting arms, has a right to affection, nurture, and tender care. However, as adoptive parents have demonstrated repeatedly, the infant accepts this mothering from any person faithful in the offering. Working mothers have fought for and are slowly gaining the right for extended maternity leaves to continue to meet the needs of their infants, but they also have discovered part-time mother substitutes for the hours while they are working. The infant's right to a mother may be more fully met by a part-time child-care worker, a baby sitter, a loving relative, or a freed-up father *and* a *renewed* mother who can give more to the child before and after meaningful employment a few hours each week.

The quality of the time a mother and child have together is more significant than the quantity of time together so long as consistent hours are shared. This is especially true if the mother feels trapped by numerous child-maintenance chores and household duties. A bedraggled housewife may spend less "quality" time with her child than a restored, revived, renewed, replenished mother who finds release and self-expression in her job. Obviously, work does not always leave one revived and replenished, but it can be a helpful diversion for weary housewives.

Poets have long extolled the bliss of motherhood as a natural female calling. Elizabeth Barrett Browning romanticized:

> Women know
> The way to rear up children (to be just),
> They know a simple, merry, tender knack
> Of tying sashes, fitting baby shoes,
> And stringing pretty words that make no sense.
> *Aurora Leigh,* Book I

William Cullen Bryant turned attention to a child's right to a mother when he wrote:

> Lord who ordainest for mankind
> Benignant toils and tender cares,
> We thank thee for the ties that bind
> The mother to the child she bears.
> ("The Mother's Hymn")

However, poets have mostly relegated to humorists the toil, pain, and frustration of child care. Harried housewives —surrounded by soiled diapers, cluttered dishes, and screaming infants—are not uncommon subjects for family cartoons. Poets who only glamorize and comics who only criticize motherhood both miss the point. Mothering is joyful *and* painful, but still a child has a right to a mother. For some mothers, this fact may mean cutting back on career goals while in the childbearing, child-rearing stage. For others, this reality could mean deciding not to have children, at least not for the present. For some housewives this actuality means finding a fulfilling job or outside recreation that brings renewed joy to the deeper aspects of the mother-child relationship.

CHILDREN HAVE A RIGHT TO A FATHER

Physical desertion by a father plagues a few mothers and their children. This painful flight from the responsibility, respect, and relationship of parenting cheats a child and often overburdens the mother. However, nearly as painful is the unavailable father who emotionally, spiritually, and psychologically deserts his children. Fathers who delegate all child care to the mother forsake their child and abandon their responsibility as fathers. They often ask "Whose children are these?" implying that since the mother physically gave birth to them, she alone should care for them. Such men flee into overextension, second jobs, or excessive traveling in order to escape parenting pressures. Some males expect their wives to tend to all needs of the offspring even though both are employed. These fathers may seek refuge in addictive drugs or alcohol, retreat into television fantasyland, or withdraw to local sports facilities and entertainment centers.

Children have a right to a father who provides for more than their financial needs. The father joins his mate in caring for the physical, educational, and recreational desires of their offspring. A father who plays with his three-month-old or three-year-old child will have a thirteen-year-old who still likes to play with him. The father meets certain protective needs for the family as he joins the mother in organizing and managing the family's daily routine. A male parent can be just as tender, affectionate, and caring as a female if he is committed to this experience. The father who provides routine care for his children builds a communication bond and strengthens the child's personal identity and development.

What we are saying is that a child has a right to parents who are committed to each other enough to share child care. Fidelity in female-male commitments is necessary for ongoing care of offspring. A child whose parent deserts can be aided by substitute parent figures and family members if these adults are faithful in ongoing relationships with the young one. Whatever the circumstance, a child has a right to a father as well as a mother. Dual-career marriages often are attacked for taking the mother from the home. We suggest that shared parenting is the optimal arrangement— even if only one spouse is employed.

For fathers this may mean revising career objectives, settling for less income, or accepting a lower standard of living in order to have quality time with the little ones. Perhaps a father could best care for his family by refusing overtime and extra jobs and caring for the home while his wife worked part time or even full time.

Pregnancy Can Be a Problem

Even when both parents are theoretically committed to dual parenting, pregnancy creates strain for working couples. An unplanned pregnancy multiplies stress and adds to the need for modification and alternatives in the couple's work habits. For some working women, an unplanned pregnancy or unwanted pregnancy may be so emotionally upsetting that they consider abortion or adoption. Some struggle to overcome resentful feelings toward what they feel is an intrusion into their careers. This certainly is not true for all "surprised" mothers. At times the father may resent the economic loss for the family when there is an unwanted conception. Planned or unplanned, the pregnancy generates problems for the working couple.

Obviously, the wife must physically adjust to her conceived condition. One issue unfolds around her physical health and consequently that of the child. At some point she will perhaps want or need to take a leave of absence before the child is born. Although most employers are generous with maternity leaves, a few find ways to terminate the employment of expectant mothers. A husband's emotional support is crucial during the prenatal development stage. One couple found that the wife could stay on the job until the week before the "due date" since the husband was willing to assume heavy responsibility for household maintenance. The couple is wise to consult a physician for specific recommendations and to put the mother's health and ultimately that of the developing infant before employment considerations. With pregnancies properly planned and integrated into a career, a woman can reduce, though not eliminate, development or work-cycle disruptions.

A second issue emerges around the father's role at the time of the delivery. Many couples find added meaning by having him participate as much as possible during the birth event. This, of course, requires time away from his job and could result in economic difficulties—especially if he is an

hourly wage earner. As social pressure mounts, more employers may be more willing to permit days off for a father at the
birth event.

A third issue arises in response to the question of how long
a mother should remain at home with the child. Of course,
the mother needs enough time to recuperate physically, but
beyond that, the father could stay with the infant unless the
mother is breast-feeding. Perhaps you recall the Iowa
mother who made national headlines by returning to her job
as a fire fighter and bringing her infant with her to the fire
station. Times have changed, and each couple will do well
to work out what fits best in their family's situation. If a
mother with a high commitment to work values is forced
into giving up her work, the child will most likely suffer.
Some women work part time for several months or years,
others take a year or more before returning to the labor
force. One creative and committed couple decided that
both the husband and the wife would work only part time
until the children were three years old.

Child-Care Alternatives Vary Widely

Economic resources directly affect alternatives for caring
for tots while Mom and Dad work. Couples who cannot
afford to pay regular help to watch the kids are resourceful
in solving their problem. Those who live close to relatives
routinely take their little ones to Mom's or Grandmother's
house. Such agreements meet with varied degrees of success.
While many relatives are willing to help out for a time, some
feel put upon, taken advantage of, and just plain "used."
Some children suffer from the instability that results from

constantly changing the place where they are "kept" while the parents labor.

For working couples who have neither close, willing relatives nor extra money, child-care choices have included trade-off arrangements, barter agreements, and available public services. One group of parents employed in shift work watched each other's offspring. Couple A left their child with Couple B during the day. In return, Couple A cared for the B children until Mrs. B came home at about 10 P.M. The fact that they all lived in the same apartment building eased transportation arrangements and permitted the children to be put to bed in their own rooms. "Not ideal, but manageable" was their reflection.

A young couple in graduate school watched their friends' child while the mother worked part time and the father was in the library. In return the father gave free music lessons to their older children. Such barter agreements benefited both couples and their children. Some two-career families have also made satisfactory child-care trade-off arrangements with retired persons in their community.

Churches, socially-minded organizations, and government programs have sporadically provided free or subsidized facilities for the children of couples with two jobs but low income. Usually such quality programs have a long waiting list or are difficult to discover.

Unfortunately, all too many infants and toddlers are left with immature school-age siblings while their mother and father eke out a living. One study reported finding "many young children, as young as five and six, being left alone for several hours every day" (O'Brian and Reckard, p. 2). A few parents defended this situation with chatter about developing early independence, but most felt insecure about the practice. We feel that the high separation anxiety of children under nine years of age makes the practice very questionable. Inadequate child care can scar tender lives and lead to years of developmental struggling.

The economic resources of two-income, middle-class families permit many to enroll their young children in private nursery school and kindergarten. Although the cost of "schooling" for their toddlers eats into the economic benefits of two salaries, the total gains seem to be sufficient. These couples have most often moved several times and do not have close neighborhood relationships or nearby relatives. The mushrooming number of new child-care facilities developed by larger churches and private groups testifies to the popularity of the nursery school solution to the child-care dilemma facing middle-class couples.

Couples who can afford to pay for child care still may have difficulty locating a quality, full-day service. A California study of one affluent community uncovered an ironic twist of events. Middle- and upper-middle-class families were seeking child care in neighboring communities where facilities had been started to help the poor. There were no all-day, all-week nursery schools available in that city.

When a wealthy husband and wife are both employed, personal child care is frequently provided by a private nurse or live-in "nanny." This ancient practice frees parents of child-rearing duties so they can pursue careers. Some parents who trust someone else to raise their offspring do spend large amounts of quality time with them. In cases where this is not true, a child is likely to develop closer bonds with the parent substitute than with the biological parents.

One last note. Some men and women sidestep what is perhaps the most difficult issue for working couples. They resolve the child-care problem by choosing to remain childless. This seems to us a legitimate, perhaps frank and honest, alternative for some couples as long as they accept the loss of the many blessings of children.

HOMEWORK AND THOSE FIRST FEW MINUTES
AFTER SCHOOL

Children are persons! Persons with hopes, dreams, feelings, and their own tasks. A child's work is creative play and learning about the world into which he or she was born. Schools help with this process but cannot be expected to do the job alone. Parents facilitate learning by signaling its importance and by overseeing homework.

Signaling the importance of learning can be done in several ways. How the day at school went, what the child did, what was learned (*if* the child is able to identify and name anything), how teachers and peers treated the child, how the child felt about the social interaction—listening to these matters not only emphasizes the fact that school and what happens there is important; it also underscores the fact that the child and what happens with the child is important. The parent cares, cares enough to listen, to "debrief" the student, receiving with interest an account of the day or the highlights of the experience. Giving time for listening and discussing reports of the school day does signal the importance of school activities, including learning.

The need even for grown-ups to recount their experiences and know someone cares about what has happened during the day is recognized in many settings. Upon completion of a workday the employed person often needs to tell someone about the experiences of the day. The traveler, returning from a journey, likes to be met by caring companions who give a feeling of interest and involvement. Likewise, the child has increased self-esteem when others show they care. The child needs to come home to a parent who listens and shares.

The child may go to an after-school program, or to a neighbor's or sitter's, or home to an older sibling, or home to emptiness. Whatever usually happens, the child needs a one-to-one experience with a listening adult; the youngster needs a caring person after the day at work: that is, school. This adult may or may not be the parent. If the child goes into the care of a nonparent, then whenever the parent and child do rejoin, the parent would do well to remember the child's needs and to question, listen, and share about the school day.

The parent may want to be aware of the child's teachable moments at other times also. A spark of interest in a certain subject can be fed with comments, discussion, appropriate books, a research trip, or time for the science experiment at home. The spark of interest can be extinguished quickly if not given fuel for energy and growth. The teachable moment for a given subject may pass quickly unless it is fed with interest and information. Working parents might be prone to be "too busy" to tend to the spark of interest and may want to be aware and alert to such possibilities; however, any parent may recognize or fail to recognize the child's interest and may or may not take the time to help the child pursue the interest.

Homework is another area in which the parents can have a direct and positive effect on the child's learning and self-esteem. The child needs physical space and many need human encouragement. The homework area needs to be conducive to study, with a reading and writing desk or table, proper lighting, comfortable temperature, paper, pencil, etc., and reasonable quietness for concentration.

Some children, days, or subjects may need more parental encouragement than others. Independent study and work habits are not natural tendencies in all children but can be learned.

Our family has a basic agreement at this time that Dad is available for questions during homework and Mom helps with proofreading later. Working parents can share homework assistance and after-school debriefing for elementary school children. They can share in the educational life of older children. Special awareness of the needs helps build a determination to make time to assist.

Identity Formation of the Child Is a Role Issue

Parents have long observed a most disturbing reality of growing children. Offspring do not develop according to what they are told about life; they emerge in patterns similar to what they see and experience with the adults around them. How many times have you already cringed when your child copied your bad habits? We still recall a few real shockers, such as repeating less-than-perfect grammar, slamming a door, and using a few questionable table manners. As children mature, they unfold along lines that reflect their parents' roles.

If Father dumps all the home care, errand-running, and child-rearing onto equally employed Mother, then the children follow suit—especially little boys in this case. We were taken aback when our twins, then only age five, sat in the family room and yelled out a short-order snack demand to their mother. When they were reprimanded, they responded almost in unison, "Well, Daddy does that and you bring him food!" Surely each parent knows the pain of seeing one's children assume negative behavior patterns and attitudes.

Identity formation—how the child sees herself or himself as a female or male—is directly related to how the child observes females and males relating in the family. This issue is especially important for dual-career parents. As we adjust to time and work pressures we need to be aware of our impact upon our children's identities. We have found that explaining new agreements and adjustments helps the young ones. Parents will want to be intentional about the impact of their changes upon their sons' and/or daughters' self-image.

Recently, after a new division-of-labor agreement between us, we failed to inform our sons. They were puzzled, confused, and uncertain at first. Finally one of them blurted out: "What's going on? Mom is outside working in the yard and you are cooking. Did you guys trade jobs again?" After we explained, they seemed satisfied. We were surprised a few weeks later by a new version of the "My dad can beat up your dad" argument. Our boys were arguing with a close friend of theirs whose mother and father are employed. One of ours said something about our switching chores and the friend replied: "I bet my mom is more liberated than your

mom. You should see all those books she has about women."
"I bet she is not . . . ," ours retorted. Certainly all three will
grow up treating women differently than those of us who
grew up with patriarchal models. Like it or not, your children will do what you do more than what you say. Their
identity will be impacted by your decisions regarding dual
or dueling careers.

Working parents of teen-agers need to be especially tuned
into their children's vocational and dating struggles. How
your adolescent sees herself or himself as a young woman or
man undergirds those tumultuous years. One girl who
watched her mother battling for the right to pursue a career
had difficulty relating to boys her own age. The daughter of
a friend of ours felt free to seek education for a male-
dominated profession because of her parents' modeling of
dual careers. A college freshman was brought for counseling
because "he showed little respect for his mother," who, in
his words, "was a drag on the family economically."

CHILDHOOD ILLNESS AND DEVELOPMENTAL STRESS

Employed parents who juggle resources to balance the
family routine are often thrown off balance by some illness
or developmental crisis of their infant, toddler, junior, or
youth.

The illness of a child disrupts the routine in addition to
causing the normal concern for health. If the child only
suffers from a minor injury, disease, or illness, one parent
may need to remain at home. Opinions may differ as to
which one should do so. Since, as one Harvard study demonstrated, usually the mother assumes major child-care duties

even when both parents are employed full time (Bryson and Bryson, *Dual-Career Couples,* p. 35), the mother is expected to take time off and be a nurse for the child. However, as more males feel comfortable in nurturing relationships, fathers decide to share in the care and comforting of ill children. One couple rotates the responsibility for "sick days" so that neither parent will jeopardize his or her employment status.

When a serious illness strikes, usually both parents want to be available to the child for the first few days. As a hospital chaplain Wade observed, however, that usually the father returned to work first. In extended cases vacation time was used and then the parents started burning the candle at both ends; that is, they would work and then return to the hospital. In a few cases the mother quit work, but both developed economic anxiety over reduced income and mounting medical costs.

Although teen-agers require less attention during times of minor illness, their needs during developmental crises loom high on any list of family priorities. For instance, one father lost nearly a month of time on his research while he "helped Tommy with advanced algebra." Another father gave up weekend overtime in order to go camping with his sons and, in their words, to "talk out some deep stuff." One mother delayed going to work for a year after the family moved so she could assist her teen-agers in some difficult adjusting to a new peer group. Another set of parents used their "sick days" to tour three college campuses with their daughter.

Dual-career parents often duel over the care and feeding of their growing children. Their children's needs are just as great as any other children's, but the time for meeting those needs may be consumed with work and resulting adjustments. We have attempted to offer a few ideas about relieving the tension of child-rearing by outlining major areas of stress and illustrating how some dual-career parents have responded. Most research that we consulted pointed to child care as the major strain on working parents. Parents help when both join in the task and each answers "Mine" to the question, "Whose children are these?"

4. Who Does the Dirty Work?

For generations women did the "dirty work" related to the three C's of cooking, cleaning, and child care. The men attended to the outside "dirty work" connected with providing the finances, protecting the family, and patrolling the animals. The Industrial Revolution affected both females and males, but women were left with a disproportionate amount of the dirty work. Except for the few remaining self-sustaining farm families, men "provide" away from the home, "protect" with electronic devices, and seldom "patrol" the animals, even pets. Of course, to the extent that their employment permits, husbands have a few routine weekend odd jobs they do such as lawn care and home repairs.

On the other hand, research suggests that running a home is just as time-consuming as ever (Savells and Cross, p. 270). Housewives still face a weekly routine of dirty work. They have modern conveniences, but these actually complicate and add to the total demands on a homemaker. More is expected by way of elegant cooking, immaculate cleaning, and effective child-rearing. When a fourth C, career, is added, the dirty work takes a lower priority.

Just what is "dirty work"? We are using the term to refer to unchanging, isolating, unchallenging, nonelective, and largely unvalued jobs. Certain tasks traditionally carried by a housewife are unchanging now and forevermore. Because they must be repeated day in and day out, with minimal variation, assignments like meal preparation and cleanup seem to many like drudgery.

The isolating nature of housework adds to the toilsome nature of a "wife's duties." Women are segregated behind the walls of their husband's "castle" with very little built-in social interaction. Most of their working husbands interact socially on the job. Assembly-line work is more bearable when the workers can share their burdens and befriend each other. Upon retreating from the stresses of the world many workers welcome "a quiet evening at home," contributing further to the housewife's social isolation.

Much of a housekeeper's job description does not challenge her intellectual, creative, or physical talents. "Anyone can do that" types of work become the "dirty work." Anyone can learn to empty trash containers, peel vegetables, clear tables, or sweep floors. Little sense of challenge comes even when cute advertising gimmicks promise that a woman will be the envy of her block for using their product. Women who spend years in the formal education process most often feel the frustration of the unchallenging grind at home. Jodi's pain made her lash out after a plodding day at home. "I did not get a master's degree to slave around like this!" she exclaimed.

When one can elect to do certain types of work, the pain of that work diminishes. However, the nonelective, forced-march element creates negative feelings about work. Early in our marriage Wade would decide to prepare a special-occasion, celebration meal for Jodi and then report: "I don't see why women complain about meal preparation. I get a kick out of fixing dinner once in a while." Later when he contracted to fix and clean up after one meal every day, rotating either breakfast or lunch, cooking became a part of his "dirty work."

Furthermore, the housewife's labor is a thankless task. Her work is largely unvalued. The incentives and rewards trickle in over the years, but there are few immediate returns to stroke her ego. For the most part she is taken for granted and made to feel guilty for not doing an even better job. All in all, contemporary society places little real value on the dirty work dimensions of home care and a family's physical maintenance. Mothering is the exception to the list of a homemaker's activities that are considered dirty work.

A few of the traditionally male tasks fall into this category, but they do not make up a high percentage of the husband's total expenditure of energy. Lawn care, auto care, and home repairs can be part of the dirty work.

As men pressure themselves into longer, overtime schedules and out-of-town travel, their dirty work is neglected or is sometimes performed by the wife. When women are gainfully employed outside the home, their dirty work might go undone. Yet the drudgery does not go away. The dual-career couple may begin to duel over "Who does the dirty work?" Some alternatives help couples to live with the stress of three full-time jobs.

Two Persons Versus Three Jobs

At least three full-time job descriptions face the dual-career couple: her job, his job, and the household jobs. Admitting that fact and defining the workload problem from that perspective are first steps in finding an answer.

A husband's job does not diminish if his wife is also gainfully employed. His work may actually seem more strenuous than if she were not employed. Many husbands and employers explicitly or implicitly expect a wife to be a support system for his job. One husband described his expectations for their home to be a sort of resource station where he made "pit stops" to recharge for the next cycle of work. A wife routinely is drafted to fix a lunchbox, pack a quick suitcase, take work-related phone calls, entertain the boss and his wife, or run errands for the company.

Traditionally, the wife of a professional man may be expected to find her life's meaning by supporting his career. The role of a minister's wife is narrowly defined by some churches. A man holding political office routinely calls upon his wife for public support. The doctor's wife often takes his phone calls at home and in some isolated rural areas may even be pressed for a quick medical opinion. When the wife is also employed, this "supportive function" fades and/or folds; then the husband wonders why he feels frustrated in his own work.

Of course, a wife's job description may likewise demand both her own energy and the support of her spouse. An interesting dynamic unfolded for a college financial aid director and her husband. When they were first married, she found a job and he did not. They rather slipped into a pattern of his keeping the house, preparing the meals, and doing the clothes while she went to work. When he finally did find a job, she complained: "It was a real shock to me. Suddenly there was nobody there doing everything, and it was a real adjustment" (O'Brian and Reckard, p. 14). This hassled working wife had enjoyed having a husband to do the dirty work. She seriously reflected: "Everyone that works needs to have a so-called traditional wife. It really frees you to be involved in your job" (O'Brian and Reckard, p. 11).

The job description of this so-called traditional wife remains as a "third job" for the both-employed couple. Few husbands and wives understand the scope of this third full-time job of household maintenance. A few of the demands include grocery shopping, everyday cooking, brown-bag-lunch-packing, household shopping, room-by-room cleaning, house-straightening, clothes-laundering, household repairing, lawn-tending, gardening, auto-maintaining, clothes-mending, child-chauffeuring, schoolwork-checking, off-to-school child-tending, child-bedtime-preparing, childhood-illness-caring, trash-disposing, emotional parenting, time-off-planning, financial bookkeeping, social-entertainment-planning, and special-help interviewing. Most likely you can expand this list with your own "dirty work."

One note of reminder may be needed at this point. We are not degrading any of these tasks. In fact, we wish to emphasize their importance to see that they do not go unnoticed in the pressure to find time for two careers. Furthermore, we do not discount persons, female or male, who find any or all of these activities rewarding. Perhaps everyone enjoys one or more of the above-mentioned descriptions. The point is that they can become the source of conflict for working couples who push them off onto each other.

Unfortunately, from our viewpoint, the working wife gets loaded with most of the household duties as early-morning or after-employment routines. Informal studies indicate that dual-career husbands help around the house less than do husbands of full-time housewives. Some husbands attempt to shame their wives into doing the dirty work. They contend that she has the freedom to work outside the home so long as she doesn't let that interfere with her "duties" as a wife and mother.

Men who are committed to their spouse's right to employment often share household duties and ultimately ease the stress of dual careers. We mentioned earlier that after the first year of adjusting routines, both-employed couples had no more stress than did marriages where the wife had never been in the labor force (Booth, p. 649).

One Tennessee couple with whom we talked were weary with their schedules. For two weeks the husband, using a time clock, kept a work log on the family. He found that, upon returning home each day, he worked an average of forty-five minutes helping with household chores. The two teen-age sons worked fifteen minutes each while the wife worked just over six hours every evening. The wife was exhausted. The boys complained that mother was always too busy to listen to them. The husband was tired of never having time to relax together. Then the family members volunteered for almost equal portions of the "third job" duties and were all happier with the results.

A myriad of solutions are possible allowing two persons to manage these three jobs. Some of the possibilities for solving the dilemma may be grouped under three headings, which will be explained in more detail. To *sort out* the dirty work, the partners may clarify priorities, lower expectations, and simplify the manner in which the work will be accomplished. Next, to *spread out* the dirty work we will give consideration to everybody's helping. Finally, to *farm out* the dirty work, not only to the partners but also to "volunteers" (other family members) and "employees" (help that is hired), may be a solution to some dirty work. Details on these possible solutions will be mentioned; maybe these possibilities will set you to brainstorming and discovering other solutions for your own situation.

Sort Out the Dirty Work

When dual-career couples are faced with an overload, they either become creative about reorganization or give up. In taking their "dirty work" seriously, some working pairs sort it out by using the *sedimentation* method. Like muddy water, muddled routines clear up when the unnecessary particles settle to the bottom. Couples are helped by bringing to the top the significant household tasks and letting those of lesser importance settle out. Like settling sand, some jobs drift to the bottom of a priority list. By examining a comprehensive list of chores, a working husband and wife can decide what is important and what is extraneous. Some aspects of the home and parenting routine will be attractive to one or both mates. These jobs rise to the surface as the "I want to do that" category.

Since each working couple has different values, interests, and family circumstances, a variety of categories may drop into the "Who cares?" category and be omitted. While one couple may decide not to have children because of their attitudes and commitments, another couple may choose not to entertain or not to hassle with clothes that need ironing; still another couple may choose to live in an apartment or a condominium and forget about lawn, shrubs, and garden.

In addition to dropping off the least important duties, a couple can sort out their dirty work by *lowering expectations.* One husband kept up the pressure for perfection. His mother had always been a compulsive cleaner who enjoyed being a full-time homemaker. His first expectations included spotless living quarters and a wife to keep it that way. His desire was matched by his wife's wishes. She even exceeded his mother in keeping their dwelling shipshape—before she found outside employment. For a while their ship appeared to be sinking. She could not work all day in her office and maintain their high standard for immaculate living. After weeks of anxiety, anguish, and arguments, they talked with a marriage counselor. After a few sessions they mutually decided that her employment was worth their accepting a little mess around the house. They reduced the pressure to clean up so much. Their lowered expectations soon felt normal and they could laugh at how compulsive their cleaning used to be. They did not omit any chores, but they settled for a lower definition of "well done."

A different approach to sorting out the dirty work focuses on *simplification.* Find an easier way to accomplish the same goal. The instant-food industry has mushroomed since wives first rushed off to the job market and had less time for the produce market. Some cleaning products are truly time-savers. By advance planning many errands can be combined into one trip. When possible, children's car pools not only save time for the chauffeurs but reduce energy consumption and save dollars. Some banks simplify financial accounting while others add to your work. When some working couples socialize together, they do not expect to be served a multicourse meal prepared by the hostess; a simple menu, potluck dinner, or just dessert will do. Instead of spending hours unsuccessfully digging out the dandelion population, spraying the weeds in minutes and watching them disappear over the next two weeks may work.

Since isolation and boredom are a part of what makes dirty work a chore, house jobs can be more pleasant when shared. The presence of another person makes the time pass faster on monotonous jobs. Some tasks, like cleaning dishes, are made for two people. Working under an automobile is facilitated by having someone nearby to hand over the tools.

Spread Out the Dirty Work

Some routine tasks just have to be done. Most couples face questions such as "Who takes out the garbage?" "Who cleans the soiled diaper?" or "Who picks up the socks?" The list of "dirty work" may include any task considered distasteful or routine. When the "dirty work" cannot be decreased, spread it out.

One obvious approach to spreading out the unattractive, repetitive, dull chores is the *division of labor* theory. Each person does an equal share and no one person has all the dirty work. A traditional husband may say to his wife, "Well, I work hard at my job, and you need to protect me from the 'dirty work' when I am at home." Maybe he does work hard, but so does she and so can they. If they do an equal share of the "third job" assignments, neither will feel unfairly overloaded.

When working couples have dual careers, everybody helps. This sharing spreads out the dirty work. When working couples duel about the jobs nobody wants to do, the dirty work piles up like a dark cloud over the family.

Even when everybody helps, the assigning of responsibilities can be a source of tension. We have discovered that the work goes better when persons can choose their assignments. Since the compulsory element contributes to making work "dirty," electing specific segments of the total responsibility reduces the negative aspects of "dirty work." After each family member has volunteered for fair portions of the total work load, the remaining tasks can be either assigned fairly according to skill and ability or delegated by casting lots or drawing straws.

A second approach to spreading out the dirty work is *rotating the jobs* that nobody likes. The change of pace spreads out the negative aspects of some jobs around the house. Recently our twins both balked at helping clear and wash the evening-meal dishes. Also, neither wanted to be first with the nightly bath. Mother came to the rescue with a rotation plan. One week J.B. takes first bath and W.C. does the dish routine with Mother; they switch for the next week. Interestingly, by the end of a week they both seem eager to switch. We also alternate some jobs and feel relief from the diversity.

Certain tasks—like telling a bedtime story, "kissing" away the hurt, and listening to after-the-date, teen-age reports—are rotated for positive reasons. We feel that, when possible, fathers and mothers should share parenting responsibilities in order to spice up the home scene. The joys of parenting fit between segments of dirty work and help to spread it out even farther.

A third line of attack for spreading out the dirty work calls for *organizing schedules*. By planning the times for family workdays, buffer zones, and diversity of assignments, it is possible to spread out the dirty work and render it manageable. One California school-teaching couple schedules Saturday morning and/or afternoon as "clean the house" day. They all join in. Even their third-grade son helps; he runs the vacuum cleaner and picks up all toys. They report that neither of them feels the pressure of housecleaning during the week because they know it will get done on Saturday. One couple had a full weeknight schedule that called for three nights of tackling the dirty work from 7 to 10 P.M. and four nights of leisure together.

Planning "buffer zones" into each day's pattern aids in spreading out those dreaded tasks. A buffer zone in the routine is like a coffee break at home. A few moments to unwind, unload, and relax helps take the edge off the household work procedure. For example, a short-order cook should not rush home to prepare the evening meal. A truck driver needs a break between work and driving a car pool of kids to the ball game. A teacher needs something between school and supervising her or his own children's homework. Buffer zones between similar tasks at home are equally satisfying. Although most workers are protective of time for a break at their employment, few practice the same wisdom in their own home.

One final approach to keeping the dirty work spread out centers on *not allowing accumulation*. Couples who learn to "do it now" experience less stress. Many tasks become "dirty work" because they are allowed to pile up. A few meals' dishes can seem like a mountain of drudgery; however, if every person helps clear the table, one or two family members can handily finish the task. Some couples answer mail and pay the bills each day as they arrive. One couple returns phone calls immediately so as to avoid keeping a list of "calls to make." By doing some jobs as they come up, you can keep the dirty work spread out.

FARM OUT THE DIRTY WORK

Dual-career couples not only sort out and spread out the dirty work, they routinely farm out certain assignments. Working couples *contract with others* for assistance with the work around the house. Couples we interviewed maintained a variety of agreements for child care, housework, laundry, meal preparation, and other routine tasks.

By far the largest group of working couples rely on help from the extended family. Of course, children do their part, but in many instances the employed husband and wife turn to their parents or grandparents in order to farm out the undone portion of the dirty work. We found that nonprofessional couples regularly turned to family members for support in maintaining two occupations; however, professional couples more often used hired help to fill in the gaps.

Portions of the professional couple's dirty work were assigned to the cleaning lady, the housekeeper, or the maid. Such extra help does not resolve all the problems. Desirable, dependable help seems to be scarce. One researcher reported that the major unresolved issue for working professional parents was settling on a satisfactory person for child-care assistance. One wife reported interviewing forty appli-cants before selecting one to look after her child (Bryson and Bryson, p. 36).

As more married pairs decide on dual careers, the need to buy assistance with the dirty work increases. Innovative re-sponses are springing up to meet that need. One lady adver-tised in the local paper, offering to be "another you" and to run errands, plan meals, do the shopping, prepare meals, or whatever was needed by a busy working wife.

A variation of the delegating approach to the dirty work is to *buy what you need* ready for consumption. Working couples eat in restaurants, cafeterias, and fast-food chains much more often than couples with only one employed person. When both partners are gainfully employed outside the home, it is more likely that they will have the laundry done professionally; buy, not make, personal gifts; and pay for routine car services.

In conclusion, we reflect upon two attitudes toward dirty work that distinguish dual-career couples from partners with dueling careers. The first is *joint ownership* of the total dirty-work load. Couples who can take a partnership ap-proach to their total "third job" assignments reduce conflict and increase productivity. On the other hand, fighting over who does whose dirty work is counterproductive. In reality, they are not "her" dirty dishes, crying children, or soiled clothes, nor is it "his" overgrown yard, under-tended garden, or out-of-gas car. If the partners claim joint responsibility for the work to be done and work together in seeing that priority areas are not ignored, then their careers are more likely to be a source of joint satisfaction.

A second attitude conducive to positive resolution of the dirty-work question is a high level of *commitment for two careers*. A key to mutually rewarding dual careers is the commitment and determination of both people that both shall be and stay employed. This commitment will lead to a plan for handling the overload and forms a mutual support system to ensure that the plan will be followed. Any load is lighter with the support of a caring other to share it. Both partners stand to gain by calling off the hassle about who does the dirty work and beginning to ponder as to how *we* can best handle the overload.

While some division of labor based on female and male roles seems universal in all cultures (Savells and Cross, p. 252), the roles of working men and women are very much in a state of change. As couples lose social sanction for any particular solution to their dirty-work problem, they must rely more heavily on their own creativity and sense of sharing.

5. Where Does All the Time Go?

For everything there is a season, and a time for every matter
under heaven:
  a time to be born, and a time to die;
  a time to plant, and a time to pluck up what is planted;
  a time to kill, and a time to heal;
  a time to break down, and a time to build up;
  a time to weep, and a time to laugh;
  a time to mourn, and a time to dance;
  a time to cast away stones, and a time to gather stones
      together;
  a time to embrace, and a time to refrain from embracing;
  a time to seek, and a time to lose;
  a time to keep, and a time to cast away;
  a time to rend, and a time to sew;
  a time to keep silence, and a time to speak;
  a time to love, and a time to hate;
  a time for war, and a time for peace.

(Eccl. 3:1–8)

The ancient authors of Wisdom Literature maintained an
almost resigned, almost casual, attitude toward the turning
of events. They concluded that God's time was little
affected by their activities, and thus, that nothing was better
than to be happy with what they were doing; a time would

occur for everything to take place in its own way. Nature both suggests and refutes such a relaxed attitude about time. One can fret and toil in the winter months and still tulips will not sprout and blossom. However, if given half a chance they will push aside any clutter and burst into fiery array when spring arrives. On the other hand, one can tend a flower garden and observe a radical improvement over simply letting nature take its course.

In a way, similar dynamics are true for the family. One seems to have little control of the cycle of family dynamics through the adjustment stage, during the childbearing and child-rearing phases, and into the empty-nest and retirement periods. The passing of time has its impact on couples. Yet, a husband and wife can take time to tend to their family and personal needs, and they can effect a great change over simply "letting things happen."

Dual-career couples may look back upon decades of lost family life and ask, "Where did all the time go?" They search for lost opportunities like naïve kittens scratching for spilled milk already consumed by thirsty dust. Furthermore, employed partners may face the frantic rush to finish a long list of "things to do today" and desperately cry, "Where does all the time go?" They search for extra minutes like reluctant children driven from the beach by oncoming rain clouds.

In this chapter we address both dimensions of the working couple's time bind, but first we consider the extra time demands of dual careers.

DUAL-CAREER TIME DEMANDS

Pure and simple overload faces working, married pairs. With just so many hours in a day and days in a week, they do not have enough time to do everything at a previously set level of satisfaction. When a husband or wife is not employed, he or she can be a backup or support person by caring for the home duties. However, when both enter the job market, time does not allow everything to continue as before. Some working men have mistakenly assumed that housewives live a life of leisure with large blocks of unused time. Consequently, when a wife joins the labor force, some husbands are surprised that time does not allow the wife to continue the same "housewifely" duties. This obvious time overload is not the only culprit.

Problems with timing turn would-be dual careers into dueling events. Timing conflicts erupt over synchronizing days off, organizing vacation time, dealing with varied work-shift conflicts, coping with overnight business trips, and scrutinizing potential moves or transfers.

When a husband and wife have different days scheduled as their workweek and consequently have different days at home, sharing becomes more difficult and weekend family trips are all but impossible. Even when a couple's normal workweek is the same, frequently they have different holiday schedules and separately recognized holidays. Persons in the medical professions, for example, often take their holidays on a staggered or rotation basis since they cannot all leave on the same day. School systems often differ in how they arrange holiday vacations. Jodi teaches in a school system that for years has taken a spring vacation several weeks before Wade's and the twins' spring break.

Similarly, vacation schedules can be difficult to organize. Some employers request that all workers take the same vacation time while operations are closed down or barely maintained. Others grant requested time for vacations based on seniority. Self-employed and professional persons often schedule vacations for slack periods and cancel them if a sudden demand for services appears. When each partner has only limited control of vacation time, planning a joint vacation can be frustrating. Unfortunately, many of the working couples that we interviewed did not regularly take a vacation but used the time off to "catch up around the house." This pattern did not seem to be as true for couples who worked together or worked for the same employer.

Although a few couples can manage working separate shifts away from the home, most seem to suffer marital disruption and increased family tension from radically different hours of employment. When children are present, the complications multiply. Functioning in dual-career settings requires planning, sharing, and attempting extra efforts at communication. When the partners are on separate schedules, they are not together enough to manage their family activities and affairs. Communication can deteriorate to only scribbled notes scattered around the kitchen in hopes that the "other half" soon will be there.

The vital balance of family functioning often teeters when one parent must be out of town overnight for business. The margin of survival is so small for most working couples that the absence of one mate swamps the family. When work requires one spouse to travel, usually the family is called upon to sacrifice, according to one study of heavy

traveling demands (Culbert and Renshaw, p. 323). If both
spouses work in high-travel jobs, family life definitely suffers.

The most critical timing issue for the couples we con-
tacted personally arose from the question, "What if one of
us changes jobs (or accepts a transfer) to an out-of-town
location?" Some couples automatically give priority to one
job, formerly or usually his. However, one contemporary
survey of a thousand working women indicated 83 percent
would ask their husband to move if the wife were offered a
better job elsewhere, and 79 percent said they felt their
husband would indeed move if asked. Two years earlier only
60 percent of the women surveyed indicated they would ask
their husbands to move and 56 percent felt the husbands
would do so (*Glamour,* p. 148). Some couples are committed to review the issues and make a joint decision. A few
said, "We try not to think of that possibility!" Professional
pairs especially anguish about relocation possibilities. One
wife, about to complete her Ph.D. in a very focused area,
wonders if she could ever find a position anywhere near her
husband's tenured, professional position. He did leave open
the possibility of moving if she had a firm offer and he could
locate "attractive possibilities" nearby.

As couples revealed how they had resolved the numerous
timing issues facing them since dual employment, a few
factors surfaced as helpful. As might be expected, commitment to each other's freedom and desire to work surfaced
again as a key factor. The ability to communicate openly,
especially in problem-solving, appeared to be important in
resolving timing stress. One final factor could be generalized
as flexibility—the ability to change with a minimal load of
stress. Couples who could "roll with the punches" and even

see the humor in their dilemma reported better adjustments in timing difficulties.

Repeatedly, researchers noted that women who worked outside the home part time reported less time-related problems. Part-time employment is an attractive option, especially while children claim their rightful share of the family's attention. Whereas one third of the working mothers in one survey reported sometimes feeling inadequate to meet both family and work demands, only one of seven mothers who held part-time jobs reported feeling inadequate to combine both roles (Savells and Cross, p. 258).

Of course, only a fragile male ego would keep a man from considering the part-time employment option also. A "red-blooded American man" could not live with himself if he only worked part time while his wife worked outside the home also—or could he? One couple we interviewed both worked part time, so they had more time for family and personal enrichment.

Practically speaking, part-time employment that pays adequately is not easy to locate. A few fortunate persons have convinced their employers to permit two persons to fill one position. Jodi is part of such an arrangement in her music teaching position. Two schools each schedule two and one half days for music instruction, and ordinarily one full-time teacher would be employed. The administrators have shown a progressive attitude, permitting two teachers to share the position. Job-sharing also functions in one other school within this system. We have received reports of secretaries, counselors, ministers, nurses, and others who function successfully in part-time and job-sharing positions. A few programs have been established to assist persons in negotiating for various types of part-time employment. However, one study indicated that organizations were likely to constrain the job freedom of wives in professional couples (Bryson and Bryson, *Dual-Career Couples,* p. 19).

Having considered some ways that dual careers make demands on a couple's time, we now turn the focus to the daily time demands of the family.

DAILY TIME DEMANDS

The demand for time each day comes from a variety of sources, but working couples seem to agree that the demand is excessive. Although each spouse finds some personal support from the job, the family has long served as the center of emotional support. The family carves out a large block of time when taken seriously. Working parents need personal time, time for sharing as a couple, time for family activities, time to resolve internal family conflicts, time to attack external family pressures, and time to communicate clearly about each of these.

Time for oneself includes attending to personal cleanliness and attractiveness; it also implies time for personal reflecting, dreaming, centering, expanding, and worshiping. In order to feel significant and appreciated as a person, each one needs this personal time block on a regular basis. After a frustrating, pressure-packed day, one exasperated working mother complained: "I have not even had time to wash my face yet today! I feel like I'm not worth anything around here!" One city dweller reported real satisfaction in taking public transportation to work each day because he had time for his personal reflection before and after the day's work routine. Time for oneself contributes greatly to a positive self-image and a sturdy personal identity.

Time for sharing as a couple means much more than, but also includes, sexual relations. In his profession Wade regularly counsels with sexually frustrated working pairs who have become too busy or too tired to experience caring, intimate time together. Sex, like meals, becomes a frantic flirting with instant substitutes, a diet bordering on malnutrition. These couples need quality time together in order to adequately meet each other's sexual needs. However, time together is important in other areas of the couple's relationship.

A marital dyad requires time to develop and maintain relational identity. When a couple begins to date seriously, they spend as much time as possible together. Often they are unaware that their relationship depends on blocks of shared time. Before matrimony they make time to be together; however, soon after they enter into a dual-career union the pattern changes. During courtship they perhaps "date" several times each week and are together most of the weekends. After living as a couple, they do not take time for dating and simply being together—especially after any children enter the picture. Chronic busyness becomes a barrier to intimacy for couples (Clinebell and Clinebell, *The Intimate Marriage*, p. 49). We encourage working couples, like other couples, to find time for at least one period each day for debriefing, to make time weekly for at least one date (dinner, lunch, theater, tennis, shopping, swimming, etc.), to find ways for occasional weekends away from it all, and to take at least one week of vacation together each year. When couples are apart, they do not support each other's emotional needs. Time together is important for continued couple growth just as time alone is significant for individual well-being.

Time alone and time as a couple need to balance with family time for overall happiness. Not only the family as a unit but each child individually demands some time from parents. Each day the family deserves some time together. This time can be simply eating an unrushed meal as a unit, having a family work project, or playing together. Family time enriches with the level of participation. For example, viewing television in the same room falls short of playing a game together, singing around the piano, or creating crafts. Each day each child merits individual attention. Working parents may find this difficult, but giving such attention is not impossible.

Remember that time exists in two dimensions—length and depth. The length or quantity of time diminishes in significance as the depth or quality of time increases. Short, uninterrupted, regular, focused time with each child can be managed if working parents are committed to its importance and use previously wasted minutes. A Purdue University family specialist feels that thirty minutes of quality family time can be more meaningful than an evening of just being present but uninvested (Denton, p. 94).

Internal family conflicts inevitably flare up and, like fires due to spontaneous combustion, they call for immediate attention. When possible, employed spouses should be alert to extinguish the flames and resolve the friction of domestic hostility. However, busy working couples cannot always stop to handle family quarrels. When the conflict cannot be addressed at once, perhaps the clash can be contained.

Families can set an appointed time to discuss the burning issues and examine alternatives to ease the pain of frustration.

Resolving internal family conflict takes time. Time is needed to listen in detail to each member's side of the problem and to redefine the problem in terms of the whole family's unity. Time is necessary to list the main alternatives for avoiding the conditions of another fiery explosion or smoldering mess. Time is essential for negotiating and evaluating the options until the family reaches a general consensus for one choice. Time is required to implement the new decision and to evaluate its effectiveness. Each stage of family conflict resolution extracts time from the family routine.

If a family does not make time for finding new and growth-producing alternatives in the midst of internal conflict, then that family will be handicapped in other areas. Unresolved conflict limits one's capacity to function as an individual, spouse, parent, and employee. Remember, as we said earlier, after the first year of the dual-career experience a couple feels less disruption in the family. If couples spent more time resolving internal conflicts during the early weeks of joint employment, their adjustment might be even quicker and smoother in the long run.

External pressures fall like crashing ocean waves upon the beachhead established by some employed spouses. Fortifying themselves and their offspring against the pounding social pressure is time-consuming as well as energy-draining. In-laws who disapprove of every child-care plan while the parents work are taking time from the couple. Age-group peers who tease and chide couples who dare to be different unknowingly hurt sensitive men and women. Unsympathetic employers who make no attempt to work out manageable assignments add to the pressure. One denominational executive assigned a husband-and-wife ministerial team to churches located two hours apart in an apparent attempt to force her back into a housewife's supportive role. Schools that only schedule parent conferences between 8:00 A.M. and 3:30 P.M. push the limits for some working couples. Government bureaucrats who expect the public to be free during the hours of eight to five, Monday through Friday, pulverize the already battered family time schedule of gainfully employed pairs who find it difficult to renew a driver's license, meet the tax assessor, or get a money order at the post office. An organization that begins weekday meetings for family members before 7:30 P.M. makes it difficult for the families where both partners work outside the home unless a meal is included in the activity. Dealing with external pressure takes time each day. Until social institutions begin to accept the fact that in over 50 percent of all married couples both partners are employed, these couples will continue to be swamped by unnecessary time demands.

Communication happens during all our waking moments, but clear, direct, and honest communication takes time. A couple needs time to communicate consistently about individual needs, couple issues, family activities, and problems to be solved. Communication is the greatest single factor affecting a person's relationship to others, according to one leading West Coast family therapist (Satir, *Peoplemaking*, p. 58). Working spouses have found it helpful to set aside regular, planned "talk it over" sessions. Each evening many couples catch up on the day's events and discuss future activities. One couple uses a few hours every Sunday afternoon with their three children present to preview the coming week. A professional couple spends the last Saturday of each month working on the next month's calendar and checking long-range expectations.

This use of time leads us to consider the long-range view of time, having examined some of the daily time demands. In the passing of the years dual-career couples may feel fulfilled or may feel some failure wondering, "Where has all the time gone?"

THE PASSING OF THE YEARS

Newly joined couples frequently harbor fantasies of sharing all areas of life. For a while they may shop arm in arm, cook meals together, and clean the apartment as a team. However, if they are both employed, a division of labor soon becomes necessary and each does some tasks alone. She may rush out for groceries while he finishes the housework, or he may run to the bank while she does yard work. If and when children enter the family scene, this trend toward separate tasks increases. Each develops specializations and the family slips into a maintenance pattern that feels comfortable. As the years pass, time is spent in continuing the pattern and in persisting with dual careers. Sometime during the middle years, perhaps when early retirement becomes an option, or the children leave home, or one partner becomes ill, the pattern is shaken and the pair reevaluate their life-style. After a period of readjustment, new time-spending patterns emerge until the retirement of both or the death of one spouse. Of course, divorce disrupts any couple's time patterns, but our experience with remarried couples points to the conclusion that without counseling and life-reorganization, a divorced and remarried person expects that the new spouse will divide the time according to an ideal of what the first pattern "should have been."

During the reevaluation and retirement adjustment of the middle years, couples fall into categories along a continuum between failure and fulfillment. Those who look back with a sense of failure are frustrated that time has not led to the rewards, fulfillments, and payoffs they expected. With various degrees of despair these couples wish they had managed the cycle of life differently. Perhaps then they would feel more positive about their relationship. Perhaps then they could feel better about their children's development as persons. Perhaps then they would find meaning in their life's work.

Dual-career couples who look back with a sense of fulfillment are the ones who early in life established priorities, set goals, and avoided the trap of materialism. A multitude of decisions that face working partners are simplified and clarified when examined by a set of mutual priorities. Employed spouses can be helped by each ranking the top five values for life. These might include children, marriage, God, money, self-expression, happiness, sports, careers, or some special mission. When decisions are weighed in balance with joint commitment to priorities, dueling sinks into the realm of time-wasting. For example, a couple committed to God, marriage, self-expression, money, and careers may not have to debate long over having children. Couples without any mutually agreeable priorities are doomed to waste large segments of time and energy.

Furthermore, couples can settle some issues by timing the long-range impact according to priorities. For example, some couples have delayed having children until both partners have established their careers, and then they limit the size of their family because careers are high on the priority list. Other families wait until the children are grown before entering a dual-career situation because children are high on their list.

New fads and strange social currents push aimless couples into blind alleys and dead-end streets of frustration. Working couples need established goals by which to gauge outside social pressure such as the partner-swapping fad of the early 1970's. Wife-swapping and swinging was touted as a way to return zest to a couple's relationship. The authors know of several couples destroyed by that illusion and have not encountered one intact couple who were helped by the experience of swinging. Couples with mutually established goals could more easily resist that call to zest because the concept did not move them toward their goal and values.

Couples caught in the materialism trap often despair for two reasons. First, they can always find someone else who has a bit more accumulated; and second, wealth does not satisfy life's deepest needs. When material goals drive working couples, they look back with a sense of missed opportunity and suspect that time has passed them by.

We feel that couples who find a goal beyond themselves and personal gains are even more likely to reflect upon the passing of years with a sense of meaning. Directional living brings value while aimless wandering breeds despair and regret. Couples whose dual careers contribute toward the creation of a better world for others find a sense of fulfillment that rises above the question, "Where have all the years gone?"

In this chapter we have examined the time pressures of dual careers, analyzed the daily time demands, and surveyed the passing of time for working couples. In the next chapter we will focus on role conflicts between men and women.

6. How Do You Tell the Men from the Women?

Traditionally, parents of a newborn infant ask two questions: first, "Is it normal and healthy?" and second, "Is it a boy or a girl?" The response to the latter question initiates different expectations almost immediately. Society sets guidelines to separate the females and the males. The hospital likely has a pink name card for a girl and a blue one for a boy. Often, clothing is selected that is for a male or a female, as the case may be. A name, which usually signals gender, is inscribed on the official birth documents. Perhaps, the baby is even touched differently. A girl may be gently stroked and treated tenderly whereas a boy may get a rougher pat and be treated aggressively. Even the traditional cigars are selected with "It's a boy" or "It's a girl" labels.

Until the child is verbal and able to differentiate behavior, few distinguishable differences between boys' behavior and girls' behavior are evident. Female and male infants learn to be dependent on a parent figure (usually mother) and adapt accordingly. However, somewhere around age three, boys learn that some new requirements go with being a male. Males are not to be passive, compliant, and dependent. On the contrary, they are expected to be aggressive, independent, and self-assertive, particularly with peers and play-mates (Udry, p. 54). Girls are not rewarded for aggressive, independent, and self-assertive behavior, because tradition-ally these have not been labeled as "feminine." After all, what are little girls made of? What are little boys made of?

School-age boys and girls are trained to play individualis-tic and competitive roles, which are similar to traditionally defined masculine roles. However, early into puberty some girls are scripted to play down their abilities when compet-ing with male peers. Although a daughter goes to school and prepares to "look after herself," parents often leave her with the hope that she will not have to use her education and training. She will not remain independent, but upon mar-riage she will turn her attention to motherhood and house-hold duties (Group for the Advancement of Psychiatry, *Treatment of Families in Conflict,* p. 299).

Our society has long made it easier for women to assume the homemaker-parent role and for men to assume a career (Savells and Cross, p. 267). For generations girls were tricked in young adulthood when they confronted a society that no longer valued them for their good performance academically but pressured them to be passive, dependent, self-sacrificing wives and mothers.

In the 1970's much of that changed. Although some women went to work only because their income was needed to support the family, some worked for other reasons. Those who did work for economic reasons appeared to remain within the traditional sex-role image for a wife and were not likely to be viewed by society as out of their role (Savells and Cross, p. 272). Those who did not seek employment out of necessity were seeking it for self-expression, personal development, and a chance to move in the mainstream of their world.

However, large segments of middle- and upper-class women who chose to be homemakers and mothers chose not to be the passive, dependent, self-sacrificing models of earlier generations. Those household engineers were products of the explosive '60s and they led supermarket boycotts, strengthened the feminist movement, read the latest psychology books on children, and stayed involved in their world.

For about half of these wives, staying involved included having a career. Conflicting reports emerge as to how well a modern, employed mother fits into her new sex role, but 51 percent of the wives in one study felt that men do not really want them to be successful at their jobs (*Glamour*, p. 149). One might conclude that the woman who chooses a career is still considered by men to be unfeminine. How does she see herself?

CAN A WOMAN DO A "MAN'S" JOB?

Women factory workers, truck drivers, college professors, miners, farmers, jockeys, law-enforcement officers, physicians, construction workers, political officeholders, attorneys, combat soldiers, ministers, journalists, business executives, and professional athletes are employed. Many are very successful, but they are placed in a sort of sociological-exception category that might be labeled "superwomen." They are considered as special women who can perform in a man's world. Considering personality traits, one can hardly tell them from men. They are hard driving, self-starting, and competitive. The question arises, "How do you tell these women from men?" The answers from some men are crude and sexist. Women are in a double bind.

A woman can do "men's" work and do it well, but she is considered by some to have lost her true femininity. She has traded her soft, fluffy, helpless image for success. Women are placed in a trap that reduces their personhood.

Women who seek a career and are married are asked to succeed in two conflicting roles. In the home they are valued for playing a passive, supporting role on behalf of their families, and on the job they are expected to be the aggressive winners who know how to take care of themselves.

In talking with some women who appear to have resolved this bind we noticed two patterns emerging. First, some women had not received pressure from their parents to be soft, passive objects of affection, but had been given consistent strokes for achievements in the competitive process. From father and mother they had learned to be caring, committed, and competitive, rather than passive from a sense of inadequacy. They had grown up with strengths from both traditional sex roles. Like traditional mothers, they were sensitive and caring, but unlike some they were also self-confident. Their giving to family members was more of an expression of commitment than a sense of oughtness. On the other hand, like traditional males, these women had developed a sense of self-confidence, competence, and competition. This new role for women has been labeled as androgynous (from *andr-*, male, and *gyn-*, female) by contemporary researchers (Savells and Cross, p. 261).

One survey found that the modern female executive is much more likely than before to fire an incompetent father even if he has two children in college. Women are more assertive now than in the past. In 1977, 70 percent said they could easily fire such a man, but in 1979 a follow-up survey found that 96 percent of the women said they would release such a male subordinate who could not do his job competently (*Glamour*, p. 149). These women were able to ask for what they needed and to fight when they did not get it.

A second pattern that we observed was a tendency toward development of a subgroup for employed wives. Married women who have a career have compared themselves to unemployed wives, unmarried, career-oriented females, and employed men, and they have felt inadequate in each category. One wife who worked forty-plus hours per week reported: "I used to feel so guilty when I thought of my neighbor. Her house was spotless, she maintained scores of rare houseplants, made many of her family's clothes, and prepared lavish meals whenever they had us over. One day it suddenly hit me that she had more time at home to do those things. I gave up trying to beat her at her game." Whenever someone raves about the accomplishments of another wife, Jodi asks, "Does she also work outside her home?" An educator reported that she was chided by other women for refusing a leadership role within their professional organization. She replied simply, "I also have a family; I will leave that extra duty for a single person." Although a flaw may appear in the presupposition that single women have more free time, the point remains that employed wives are developing a subgroup for personal validation. As this group identity expands, the social double bind for women may well diminish and perhaps someday nobody will ask if a wife can do a "man's" job.

One interesting note appeared in research with wives from professional pairs. When wives and their husbands were both psychologists, you may recall that these women were more successful in their careers than unmarried female psychologists (Heckman, Bryson, and Bryson, "Problems of Professional Couples," p. 330).

CAN A MAN DO A "WOMAN'S" JOB?

Having asked such a question, we might be expected to discuss men as nurses, secretaries, preschool teachers, or domestic helpers but, while men are doing well in these fields, our focus is more on the need for male liberation. Men, like women, have traditionally been cast into narrow sex-role categories. They were considered failures if they did not meet the standard. Men who were not winners in the macho-male area of athletics and in traditionally male vocations were pushed aside as effeminate, unmanly, and weak. Wade grew up with early participation in competitive sports in a small Midwestern community. He had a leadership-oriented, successful father and a caring, giving mother. When Jodi entered the job market, the big question for Wade surfaced, "Can a man do a woman's job (and still be a man)?" He meant, "Can a man be caring and giving?" As we have interviewed husbands of dual-career pairs, we have discovered this to be a common concern. Giving, as in housework, has traditionally been called "women's work."

Men who are raised to be "rough and tough and hard to bluff" go through a period of self-doubt when they begin to join in housework and child care. When his wife works, a man may rationally recognize the fairness of sharing domestic responsibilities, but emotionally the shift creates pain. One husband whose wife had gone to work recalled: "The first time I got up and fixed breakfast for the family I felt awful. I thought to myself that a real man would not be doing something like this. I even entertained the idea that divorce would be a better alternative than being 'hen-pecked.' "

Even emotional sensitivity, responding to a child's hurts, has been outside the traditional role of a father. While his wife was at work, one man had cleaned and bandaged his son's bike-accident scratches. He then held the seven-year-old wounded racer until the boy sobbed himself to sleep. Later in recounting the story the father said, "I guess I made a pretty good mother." In fact, he had been a caring, sensitive male parent, but he just could not incorporate these characteristics into his sex-role image as "father." He disassociated the care-giving from his own identity by labeling it as mothering.

The men that we interviewed who reported being content about being in a dual-career marriage seemed to be comfortable with being caring, giving persons. They even felt a sense of pride that they were able to make room for two careers within one family structure.

Like women, a group of men appear to be liberated toward being androgynous. They find self-affirmation in being sensitive, caring, and competent. Also, they may be developing a subgroup of working men whose wives are employed. They can be observed comparing how many hours they spend doing housework and how much time they have for their children. One man, whose wife no longer worked outside the home, apologetically explained to his male peers:

"She chose to quit work. I was very willing to make a go of dual careers."

If both men and women develop the best characteristics from traditional sex roles, how will you tell the androgynous men from the androgynous women? The answer may well be, "Who cares?" If men and women can function as persons, partners, and parents, what difference does it make how they cease the duel and begin to function as dual-career couples? We trust that the physical differences can stand as sufficient to separate the sexes. The women are the ones who have female sex organs and bodily functions; the men are those who have male sex organs and bodily functions. Each sex is equally good. A person's job does not make that person female or male. Most jobs can be done equally well by an androgynous female or an androgynous male.

The couples that we encountered seemed to divide along laboring lines in their receptivity to men and women doing the same jobs. The men doing manual labor and hazardous jobs seemed reluctant to accept women in their trade—or to accept men who were caring and giving. These working-class males accepted a woman's right to be employed mostly when her help was needed to supplement the family income as, for example, to make a major purchase, pay unexpected medical expenses, or assist with the children's educational expenses. Men in management, sales, and service-oriented occupations appeared to us more receptive to the concepts of androgyny.

Evidence from a New York study did not indicate rivalry or envy on the part of professional husbands whose wives were playing the dominate-career role (Bryson and Bryson, *Dual-Career Couples,* p. 38). These men were able to maintain a strong self-image while identifying with their partners in mutual support of the family.

EQUAL PAY FOR EQUAL WORK?

Money and earning power support the value ascribed by society to occupations. In Russia, for example, the medical doctors generally are not highly valued and not well paid, and are mostly females. The case is otherwise in most American communities, where medicine is a male-dominated field. In many occupations, women have traditionally been guided into supportive, nonleadership roles such as nursing, typing, and teaching. They are promoted more slowly than equally competent males. As recently as 1976, actresses discovered that only a small proportion of leading roles had been written for women. Most major productions called for male stars and female supporting roles. Some institutions defended lower pay scales for women by rationalizing that men were most likely to be the sole support for a whole family while women were usually either single or adding income to an already existing source of basic support.

Women's income is rising in comparison to that of equally qualified men but has not attained the same level. Most women in 1978 were still at a disadvantage in poorly paid jobs that were tagged as "women's work" according to an administrator for the Women's Bureau of the United States Labor Department (*Progress Bulletin*, p. 1). The Labor Department indicated that even as late as 1978 the average salary paid to women was just over half that earned by men. Even at a younger level, girls baby-sit with human lives for much less per hour than boys receive for doing yard work with inanimate objects.

We noticed an odd contradiction in men's responses that could best be summarized thus: "I want my wife to be paid as much as any man doing the same type of work, but I can understand why women in my area of work are not paid as much as men." Often such reflections were explained in terms of women taking time from the career cycles to tend to children or having been latecomers to the field. Perhaps in some cases women choose to make commitments that reduce their long-range promotion rate, but could not men equally do so? We suspect power needs feed the continuing battle of the sexes.

POWER AND SEX ROLES

Popular, self-proclaimed religious prophets have focused on authority and power as key dynamics for "saving the crumbling American family." A few have constructed hierarchical models for male dominance over females based on a peculiar interpretation of the New Testament teachings of Paul. A few radical feminists who stress separation of the sexes so that women can claim their powerful identity seem in some cases to be suggesting a return to a society where women hold all the power.

We can imagine that for an occasional insecure woman, a dominating husband who makes her submissive might stabilize a shaky situation temporarily while the couple consolidate matters or get their act together. However, as general solutions for peace between the sexes, domination by one sex on the one hand, and the separation of the sexes on the other, appear to be oversimplistic power plays.

Working outside the home does bring more power to women of low-income families who otherwise are totally dependent on their husbands. Middle- and upper-class women who already have some degree of family power frequently express their power by choosing to pursue a career. Power brings them work rather than work bringing them power. Conversely, men whose wives work out of financial necessity feel threatened by a loss of power, while men whose wives choose to work for other reasons do not feel as threatened.

These feelings seem to us to indicate that the key issue is one of resolving the power struggles—not of defining sex roles in terms of employment. We have tested a model for mutually shared power based on commitment, not self-service. Couples on retreats and in conferences have responded positively to viewing the New Testament passage in Ephesians 5 as a foundation for resolving the power fight.

Be subject to one another out of reverence for Christ. Wives, be subject to your husbands, as to the Lord. For the husband is the head of the wife as Christ is the head of the church, his body, and is himself its Savior. As the church is subject to Christ, so let wives also be subject in everything to their husbands. Husbands, love your wives, as Christ loved the church and gave himself up for her, that he might sanctify her, having cleansed her by the washing of water with the word, that he might present the church to himself in splendor, without spot or wrinkle or any such thing, that she might be holy and without blemish. Even so husbands should love their wives as their own bodies. He who loves his wife loves himself. For no man ever hates his own flesh, but nourishes and cherishes it, as Christ does the church, because we are members of his body. "For this reason a man shall leave his father and mother and be joined to his wife, and the two shall become one flesh."

(Eph. 5:21–31)

Power of the kind introduced by Jesus was not earthly dominance. Rather than lead a military revolution to compel persons to follow his beliefs, Jesus spearheaded a revolution beginning within persons, one that led them in his path. His key was sacrificial love. He so sacrificially loved his followers, the church, that he died for them. They so loved in response to his leading.

Husbands and wives who likewise sacrificially love their spouses will experience a new spirit of cooperation. The act of self-giving suspends the "one up" and "one down" power struggle and redefines the relationship in terms of equity. The mate who honestly asks first, "How can I use my gifts as a person to meet my partner's needs?" will have a mate who no longer is interested in having power as the right to force need-meeting behavior. When both sexes begin to focus on using their gifts to respond to the needs of the other, then power will rest with the givers as a natural result of the commitment to give. Then we would no longer distinguish the men from the women by which ones have the power and which ones get oppressed.

Same-Profession Couples

For generations couples worked side by side on the farm or in a small family shop; now some professional couples toil shoulder to shoulder in the medical center, the local church, the research laboratory, the office building, or the classroom. Couples who meet and marry while in specialized graduate programs or professional schools often choose to become a team in work and employment as well as "in sickness and in health. . . ." We talked with a few such couples and were impressed with their ingenuity for curtailing personal competition between themselves and for working as a team striving for some common goal. Same-profession couples who chose to work together seemed sincerely committed to nourishing both careers. They were not concerned regarding which one generated the most income, but usually the man did so. They felt more productive as individuals in a profession because they were a team.

The ability to support and understand each other during job stress resulted in fewer times of job-related depression, according to one professor. A researcher noted that being able to discuss issues in detail at work and at home generated insights faster for her. She continued to note that husband and wife stimulated each other intellectually by challenging new ideas and forced each other to develop comprehensive support for those ideas.

One clergy couple served the same church and rotated some duties. Other tasks were divided according to special gifts. They shared the preaching, worship leadership, and general visitation. She took the lead in visiting the sick, counseling, and administration; he took a major role in music and education.

Some problems other than the obvious area of competition still face same-profession couples. One area was finding time alone. Each person needs some time alone and often work or commuting to work provides one major outlet for individual time. Couples who are employed together may have less desire for time together at home.

A second problem area was the tendency to see the world from only one focused, limited perspective. They were so dedicated to one area, their profession, that they failed to relate to the world in a broader perspective. They lived their profession and could talk of little else.

A third problem was their team power in professional circles. They were treated either as one person with double voting power or as two persons with a single voting privilege. This was painful for them at times and for their professional colleagues at other times. Some institutions still will not employ couples because of these stresses.

In conclusion, this chapter has looked at the changing sex roles of men and women and has pointed toward functioning that does not depend on femaleness or maleness but on the abilities and interests of well-rounded persons. Equity for each spouse will suspend the struggle for power and focus each partner's attention on her or his level of commitment to meet the mate's needs.

The final outcome for dual-career couples depends not only on their adjustments but also on the social context of their family. The social realities need to change in order for couples to function fully with two occupations. Employers and the business world will have to adjust to the significance of the family before some stress can be relieved. Domestic laws need to be refined in areas that limit women. As the society adjusts to the presence of working couples, then working couples will experience less dueling.

One institution that can help bring about needed social

change and aid dual-career couples in coping with their stress is the church. As members of a congregation, you can help yourself and other working couples. Our concluding chapter will focus on specific ways you as the church can aid dual-career partners.

7. The Church's Response to Employed Couples

The complexity of Western society necessitates interaction between elements such as church, family, legal system, educational system, and economic system. While no one system can control the others, each does have an impact on the others. A rise in the inflation rate threatens family life, and a deterioration of family life reduces an employee's capacity on the job. A shift in school hours to adjust to forced busing changes a family's capacity to manage two adult careers outside the home, and a loss of family support for a student soon shows in the classroom. Some changes in the tax laws would be felt in most churches. Liberation theology, as set forth by blacks, women, and Latin-American theologians, has been felt by numerous governmental structures.

This chapter focuses on the contributions of one institution, the church, toward aiding dual-career husbands and wives. It calls upon dual-career couples to direct their church's ministry to help dueling career couples. The church cannot expect to resolve all career duels. Changes in the legal, economic, social, educational, and medical structures of society must accompany the church's response. While individual church members, churches, and church organizations can work to effect changes through these other elements of society, they can do some things themselves. Before we two-career families ask our churches to declare holy war on the blind spots in society, we Christians must first examine the beams in our own eyes.

FOCUS ON FAMILY LIFE

A first step for denominations, as well as for the individual church, is to accept some responsibility for the quality of family life, not only for its members but also for the larger social network. Until recently the World Council of Churches resisted establishing a Department of Family Ministry (Mace and Mace, *Marriage Enrichment in the Church,* p. 44). It was only in the 1970's that large denominations such as the Roman Catholic, Presbyterian, Methodist, and Baptist churches began to offer wide-scale programs for families. Resistance from church leaders focused on protecting the privacy of family life and directing the church's resources toward more pressing issues. Both these ideas miss the point of the interconnectedness of society. The church cannot afford to neglect the general quality of family life. Families cannot afford to be ignored by churches.

A general focus on family life will soon involve churches in the issues facing couples who work for pay. Churches will hear the painful cries of hurting family members and see the suffering of men and women trapped by outmoded role concepts. Churches can offer the New Testament messages as hope for the enslaved hordes of repressed people. In Christ there is no male and female (Gal. 3:28). Jesus broke the social fetters of his environment and treated women as persons (Stagg and Stagg, p. 113). The church can defend the right of women to choose to work for remuneration, to work at home, or to elect some combination of both. We feel that women have the right to work at home, for employment, or as volunteers, and that the church can be a defender of that right. Dual-career couples, and not just women, need to take the lead in calling the issues to the attention of their church leadership.

Men have been just as imprisoned as women but in different roles. Churches can help liberate men to be caring, giving, feeling persons. Jesus led his disciples to be examples of men free from the narrow restrictions that typed men as uncaring, selfish, nonfeeling individuals who must be aggressive, successful, and always self-confident. As the churches focus on supporting expanded options for females and males, much of the unnecessary guilt that shackles dual-career couples will fall by the wayside.

However, the freeing of choices creates another problem for modern men and women. How do they choose among the various options? As the alternatives expand, so does the confusion. By what values does an individual, or a couple, evaluate questions from the contemporary scene? One limited benefit of the traditional "men work outside and women work inside the home" concept of normal was that it virtually eliminated anxiety about what one was to do. Now persons must decide for themselves. Do I seek a career? Do I remain single or get married? Do I want to commit myself to a child? Do I work part time or full time? Do I work while the children are young? Couples are faced with questions of what to give up and what to pursue.

The church can clarify and teach values by which the

multitude of decisions can be evaluated. By focusing on theological and Biblical values the religious community offers working couples guidelines for decision-making. Unless the working couples take the lead in calling the churches to this task, the churches are not likely to respond.

One researcher concluded that in some social settings dual-career families are still considered a questionable and variant social pattern (Rapoport and Rapoport, *Dual-Career Families,* p. 313). Because of the power of religious institutions to validate as well as to question values, the church's attitude toward working couples is very important. When religious leaders openly accept and work for the rights of couples to choose dual careers, then general acceptance of spouses who are both employed will increase. The church can assist couples in clarifying why they want to be in dual careers and examine motivations in the light of Christian values.

One final area of focus for family life comes as a spin-off of the church's stance toward change. Generally, the churches have been slower to adopt new social patterns and have served a valuable stabilizing role for Western society. However, unless a church is clear about the principles by which changes are evaluated, confronted, and/or encouraged, couples may sense a general attitude of resistance to family change itself. A serious focus on family life needs openness in attitudes about flexibility. A couple's ability to change—that is, to roll with the punches—greatly enhances their likelihood of succeeding in dual careers (Bryson and Bryson, *Dual-Career Couples,* p. 78). The church can support an open stance for couples facing the complex decisions about work. In fact, a church's support during periods of change may make the difference between adjustment and family disaster. Again, couples who are employed may have to initiate this process within the churches.

Examining Our Own House

Some couples that we interviewed were critical of the Judeo-Christian tradition and the church as they had experienced it. As we Christians examine our own house, we see the need for a cleaning operation. As we cast out some evils, we must remain alert to replace them with positive elements, lest a multitude of evils take their places. What can you as a dual-career couple do about any negative elements in your church?

The first element that can work family evil from within a church is *unbalanced time demands.* A church may demand too much time from a few families or plan activities without coordination. Usually in the first instance guilt is projected upon some sensitive family, and the members respond by accepting an overload. We know of one couple that has seven important positions of responsibility in their church. Both partners are employed. They complain of never having any time for family life. The unbalanced time demand from their church can be an evil force from a virtuous intention. Also, they feel more guilt, not less. The husband said that he could not adequately manage his four areas of church responsibility and "felt bad" that he could not give more time. Certainly, a church and its families would both profit if couples were permitted only one area of responsibility and that within the dimensions of their available time.

Traditionally, wives who chose not to be employed have voluntarily labored long hours for their churches. As more women choose to be employed, the free voluntary source of church labor will lessen. Churches may be tempted to overload the faithful few until these also give up or burn out. Consuming the faithful by overload is like eating the seed corn. If the faithful could be used to enlist more helpers for less time, then the churches would be more stable and couples could also be under less overload. Enough about overload. What about unbalanced activities?

A dual-career couple especially needs a church that does not expect its working couples to waste time running to and from the church. There are alternatives. Several churches plan many activities for the family, but all on the same night. Preschoolers, children, youth, and adults come together for a fellowship meal and then disperse for an hour or so of Bible study, music, mission emphasis, prayer groups, or recreational activities. A church that plans activities every night of the week may intend well but will not meet the needs of the family when both parents work.

Stop. Think a moment of the working couples in your church. Do they experience unnecessary pressure from overload or unbalanced scheduling? What can you do about it? Have you brought this to your minister's attention? Can you help your church cast out time-related evils and replace them with balanced job distribution and coordinated activity scheduling?

As Christians examine their own house they will find a second element that can work evil for families—that of *restrictive attitudes* about females and males. One woman felt strongly that her church was a destructive element in society. She and her husband were happy with their dual-career patterns, but her church taught that women are inferior to men and suggested that women should only have one role in life, that of being a supportive wife and mother. She strongly objected and felt she could no longer worship in that setting. Her husband was troubled by their loss of intimacy about spiritual matters and felt uneasy when he went to church without her. He also had negative feelings about the implied teaching of their church that the husband should be the sole family leader. He did not like that pressure to win. He felt that his church oppressed men as well as women.

The evil of restrictive attitudes about females and males needs to be replaced by a full theology of persons based on both the Biblical teachings and the attitudes of Jesus toward men and women. Pause and reflect for a moment. Can you summarize what your particular faith group implicitly or explicitly teaches about men and women? Do you agree? Does this help or hinder family life within your community? What can you do to support or confront these attitudes?

A third element of evil from some churches and religious organizations stems from *discriminatory practices* affecting dual-career clergy couples, i.e., couples in which the minister's wife (or husband) also is employed outside the home. Some churches pressure their pastor's spouse to refrain from outside employment. Actually, they want the spouse to work for the church as a full-time volunteer. One church was interviewing a prospective staff minister and someone blatantly asked him, "How much time can we expect each week from your wife, and is she musically talented?" The practice of paying one member of a family and "employing" the total family appears unfair at best and sinful at worst.

We talked with a few clergy couples and uncovered a pit of hostility toward denominations that discourage or refuse dual careers within their system. This feeling was especially true in churches that openly supported women's rights for equal-employment opportunities but only in so-called secular fields. Such churches spot the alien speck but miss the beam from their own point of view. Some churches refuse to ordain women or are reluctant to employ women but accuse business and industry of bias if they do not provide equal opportunities for men and women.

Hard data were not available to support one husband's accusations against churches, but we suspect he may be closer to the truth than we had previously thought. He charged that churches and church colleges employ large numbers of women at below-standard wages and in some cases find legal loopholes to employ student wives at below the minimum wage. If he is correct, the actions of these groups will drown out any ethical proclamations from their teachings about families, dual careers, and working women.

We Christians must cast out the evils in our own house and replace them with congruent pronouncements and practices. If churches can be supportive of dual-career families, then much of the social dueling will abate. How can you confront and/or support your church's practice of treating men and women as persons?

CHURCH PROGRAMS FOR EMPLOYED COUPLES

For centuries the church has responded to unmet needs of groups of hurting persons. In the Middle Ages, medicine was often a function of religious orders. Many American hospitals were founded by faith groups. Educational centers were first established with religious resources. Even much of our legal system is based on Christian morals. The pattern has been for the institutions to develop and become autonomous or become a part of government. Few hospitals take more than their name and chaplain from a religious group. Great colleges stand on their own with only limited denominational involvement. In some cases they are not even recognized as denominational institutions. Recent trends appear to be toward widening the gap between the church and government.

However, with each major social change come new areas of need and, thus, new opportunities for the church to respond. We would like to suggest a few programs and services that couples, as members, could initiate through their church which might help alleviate dual-career pains.

From within the church's program could come a structure for family life education. In addition to including family life issues in the regular teaching and preaching ministry, a church might schedule a family life week or weekend with special conferences and outside speakers. We know many churches that make this an annual event—often in May. Many general topics are covered, such as children, commitment, communication, conflict resolution, and caring; or the focus may be on the needs of special groups, such as single parents, widows, and working couples.

A second program that could help meet the needs of working couples would be couples enrichment and growth groups. Groups of four to six working couples can meet together regularly, perhaps weekly, for sharing on issues of mutual concern. These groups have been especially helpful during that first year of major adjustment to the dual-career status. A very useful book in beginning such groups is Howard Clinebell's contribution, *The People Dynamic*. Consciousness-raising groups for men, women, or couples can help a church to share its values about related issues at a personal level and encourage social action and mission action among its members. *Counseling for Liberation* by Charlotte Holt Clinebell (still married but now legally named Charlotte Ellen) has provided a lively point of departure for issues related to women who work outside their homes.

A third supportive program would be couples retreats. In addition to providing helpful content, a church-based working couples retreat provides the structure for some quality time together. We suggest that couples plan such retreats with a resource couple, not one individual. Some churches are already making this an annual event. The more popular retreats leave plenty of unstructured couple time but provide stimulating information and issues for consideration.

A fourth program for churches is premarital counseling for couples. Although many pastors are involved in premarital care and counseling, they seldom discuss career-related issues and almost never involve the bride and groom with other couples. Married couples can be involved with the minister in preparing others for marriage. One program that we liked involved three married couples, one of which had dual careers, and three couples-to-be. They met for two evenings in each of the married couples' homes and discussed prearranged topics like money, sex, power, communication, religion, in-laws, and role expectations. In addition to providing helpful content, these groups created lasting friendships for new couples and often cut across generation barriers.

Two services to working couples that some churches have provided are still greatly needed. Perhaps the number one need of working parents is for adequate child-care facilities. Churches usually have unused weekday space that can be used for child-care programs, not only for preschool children but also for after-school care of elementary school children. Most working parents can afford to pay for child care, but some need help as a mission effort of the congregation. Of course, other families need adequate child-care programs— especially one-parent families. Not only do such services aid dual-career spouses, but they provide a point of contact between couples and the church as well as offering a Christian environment to the children.

A second need is for a crisis counseling service. The dueling couple often looks for marriage and family counseling from the minister. Even though more ministers are being introduced to counseling as a part of their seminary education, most are not taught to be in-depth counselors. Some churches have employed trained ministers of counseling. Others have jointly sponsored pastoral counseling centers where they can refer couples for help in times of crisis. Churches that reach out to couples in crises find eager couples who respond with gratitude.

Now review these suggested church programs for two-career couples. Are you getting what you need from your church? Are you doing your part to help others with what they want and need? How can you get involved? With your minister begin a dialogue about these issues.

Our intention in the preceding pages has been to raise issues and to offer alternatives, not to suggest any one model for all two-career marriages. We hope that in a context of mutual commitment and open communication each couple will call off any career dueling and create their unique dual-career model.

Bibliography

BOOKS

Achtemeier, Elizabeth. *The Committed Marriage.* Westminster Press, 1976.

Bird, Caroline. *The Two-Paycheck Marriage.* Rawson, Wade Publishers, 1979.

Bryson, Jeff B., and Bryson, Rebecca B. (eds.). *Dual-Career Couples.* Human Sciences Press, 1978.

Clinebell, Charlotte Holt. *Counseling for Liberation.* Fortress Press, 1976.

———. *Meet Me in the Middle.* Harper & Row, 1973.

Clinebell, Howard J. *Growth Counseling for Mid-Years Couples.* Fortress Press, 1977.

———. *The People Dynamic.* Harper & Row, 1972.

——— and Clinebell, Charlotte Holt. *The Intimate Marriage.* Harper & Row, 1970.

Conger, John Janeway. *Contemporary Issues in Adolescent Development.* Harper & Row, 1975.

Denton, Wallace. *Family Problems and What to Do About Them.* Westminster Press, 1971.

Dobson, James. *Dare to Discipline.* Tyndale House Publishers, 1970.

Duvall, Evelyn Millis. *Evelyn Duvall's Handbook for Parents.* Broadman Press, 1974.

Frankl, Viktor. *Man's Search for Meaning.* Beacon Press, 1963.

Group for the Advancement of Psychiatry. *Treatment of Families in Conflict.* Jason Aronson, 1970.

Howell, John C. *Growing in Oneness.* Nashville: Convention Press, 1972.

Mace, David, and Mace, Vera. *Marriage Enrichment in the Church.* Broadman Press, 1976.

—— and ——. *We Can Have Better Marriages.* Abingdon Press, 1974.

McConnell, Taylor, and McConnell, June. *A Family Life Style in a Changing World.* Nashville: Graded Press, 1975.

Oates, Wayne E. *Confessions of a Workaholic.* World Publishing Co., 1971.

——. *On Becoming Children of God.* Westminster Press, 1969.

—— and Rowatt, Wade. *Before You Marry Them.* Broadman Press, 1975.

Rapoport, Rhona, and Rapoport, Robert. *Dual-Career Families.* Penguin Books, 1972.

Satir, Virginia. *Conjoint Family Therapy.* Rev. ed. Science and Behavior Books, 1967.

——. *Peoplemaking.* Science and Behavior Books, 1972.

Savells, Jerald, and Cross, Lawrence J. *The Changing Family.* Holt, Rinehart & Winston, 1978.

Shorter, Edward. *The Making of the Modern Family.* Basic Books, 1975.

Smart, Mollie Stevens, and Smart, Laura S. *Families: Developing Relationships.* Macmillan Publishing Co., 1976.

Stagg, Evelyn, and Stagg, Frank. *Woman in the World of Jesus.* Westminster Press, 1978.

Udry, J. Richard. *The Social Context of Marriage*, 3d ed. J. B. Lippincott Co., 1974.

PERIODICALS

Adams, Bert N. "Ethical Issues Facing the Contemporary Family," *Review and Expositor*, 75:1 (Winter 1978), 105–114.

Arnott, Catherine C. "Husbands' Attitude and Wives' Commitment to Employment," *Journal of Marriage and the Family*, 34:4 (Nov. 1972), 673–684.

Barnette, Henlee. "Coarchy: Partnership and Equality in Man-Woman Relations," *Review and Expositor*, 75:1 (Winter 1978), 19–24.

Bebbington, A. C. "The Function of Stress in the Establishment of the Dual-Career Family," *Journal of Marriage and the Family*, 35:3 (Aug. 1973), 530–537.

Booth, Alan. "Wife's Employment and Husband's Stress: A Replication and Refutation," *Journal of Marriage and the Family*, 39:4 (Nov. 1977), 645–650.

Bould, Sally. "Female-Headed Families: Personal Fate Control and the Provider Role," *Journal of Marriage and the Family*, 39:2 (May 1977), 339–349.

Bruce, John Allen. "Intergenerational Solidarity Versus Progress for Women?" *Journal of Marriage and the Family*, 38:3 (Aug. 1976), 519–524.

Bryson, Rebecca; Bryson, Jeff B.; Licht, Mark H.; and Licht, Barbara G. "The Professional Pair: Husband and Wife Psychologists," *American Psychologist*, 31 (Jan. 1976), 10–16.

Burke, Ronald J., and Weir, Tamara. "Relationship of Wives' Employment Status to Husband, Wife, and Pair Satisfaction and Performance," *Journal of Marriage and the Family*, 38:2 (May 1976), 279–287.

————— and —————. "Some Personality Differences Between Members of One-Career and Two-Career Families," *Journal of Marriage and the Family*, 38:3 (Aug. 1976), 453–459.

Cadden, Vivian. "The Good, Good Money and the Pride," *Working Mother*, 2:1 (May 1979), 65–67.

Chadwick, Bruce A.; Albrecht, Stan L.; and Kunz, Phillip R. "Marital and Family Role Satisfaction," *Journal of Marriage and the Family,* 38:3 (Aug. 1976), 431–440.

Culbert, Samuel A., and Renshaw, Jean R. "Coping with the Stresses of Travel as an Opportunity for Improving the Quality of Work and Family Life," *Family Process,* 11:3 (Sept. 1972), 321–337.

Cutright, Phillips. "Income and Family Events: Family Income, Family Size and Consumption," *Journal of Marriage and the Family,* 33:1 (Feb. 1971), 161–173.

Farkas, George. "Education, Wage Rates, and the Division of Labor Between Husband and Wife," *Journal of Marriage and the Family,* 38:3 (Aug. 1976), 473–483.

Felson, Marcus, and Knoke, David. "Social Status and the Married Woman," *Journal of Marriage and the Family,* 36:3 (Aug. 1974), 516–521.

Glamour. "How Working Women Feel NOW About Jobs, Men, Salaries," *Glamour,* 77:2 (Feb. 1979), 148–149.

Heckman, Norma A.; Bryson, Rebecca; and Bryson, Jeff B. "Problems of Professional Couples: A Content Analysis," *Journal of Marriage and the Family,* 39:2 (May 1977), 323–330.

Hicks, Mary W., and Platt, Marilyn. "Marital Happiness and Stability: A Review of the Research in the Sixties," *Journal of Marriage and the Family,* 32:4 (Nov. 1970), 553–574.

Hudis, Paula M. "Commitment to Work and to Family: Marital-Status Differences in Women's Earnings," *Journal of Marriage and the Family,* 38:2 (May 1976), 267–278.

Marciano, Teresa Donati. "Middle-Class Incomes, Working-Class Hearts," *Family Process,* 13:4 (Dec. 1974), 489–502.

Oates, Wayne E. "The Psychosocial Dynamics of Family Living," *Review and Expositor,* 75:1 (Winter 1978), 67–74.

Rapoport, Rhona, and Rapoport, Robert N. "Men, Women, and Equity," *The Family Coordinator,* 24:4 (Oct. 1975), 421–432.

———— and ————. "The Dual-Career Family: A Variant Pattern and Social Change," *Human Relations,* 22 (Feb. 1969), 3–30.

Rosen, Benson; Jerdee, Thomas H.; and Prestwich, Thomas L.

"Dual-Career Marital Adjustment: Potential Effects of Discriminatory Managerial Attitudes," *Journal of Marriage and the Family*, 37:3 (Aug. 1975), 565–572.

Safilios-Rothschild, Constantina. "The Influence of the Wife's Degree of Work Commitment Upon Some Aspects of Family Organization and Dynamics," *Journal of Marriage and the Family*, 32:4 (Nov. 1970), 681–691.

Scanzoni, John. "Gender Roles and the Process of Fertility Control," *Journal of Marriage and the Family*, 38:3 (Aug. 1976), 677–691.

———. "Sex Role Change and Influences on Birth Intentions," *Journal of Marriage and the Family*, 38:1 (Feb. 1976), 43–58.

Szinovacz, M. E. "Role Allocation, Family Structure and Female Employment," *Journal of Marriage and the Family*, 39:4 (Nov. 1977), 781–791.

White, Ernest, "Biblical Principles for Modern Family Living," *Review and Expositor*, 75:1 (Winter 1978), 5–17.

White, L. C. "Maternal Employment and Anxiety of Mother Role," *Louisiana State University Journal of Sociology* (Spring 1972).

OTHER

Loper, Mary Lou. "Women Make Sacrifices for School, New Careers," *Los Angeles Times*, Part IV (Jan. 23, 1979), pp. 1–3.

Mills, Liston O. "When Both Parents Work" (cassette tape), Nashville: Broadman Records, 1977.

O'Brien, Thelma, and Reckard, Scott. "Two Heads Are Better than One?" *Upland Courier*, Upland, Calif. (Feb. 1, 1979), pp. 1–15.

Progress Bulletin. "Women's Salaries: Only Fifty Percent of Men's," *Progress Bulletin*, Pomona, Calif. (March 17, 1979), p. 1.